ODAR

BOOK ONE

JIDO

**Denice Peter
Karamardian**

ODAR

other; stranger; foreigner
(in the Armenian language)

JIDO

grandfather;
(in an Arabic dialect of Syria)

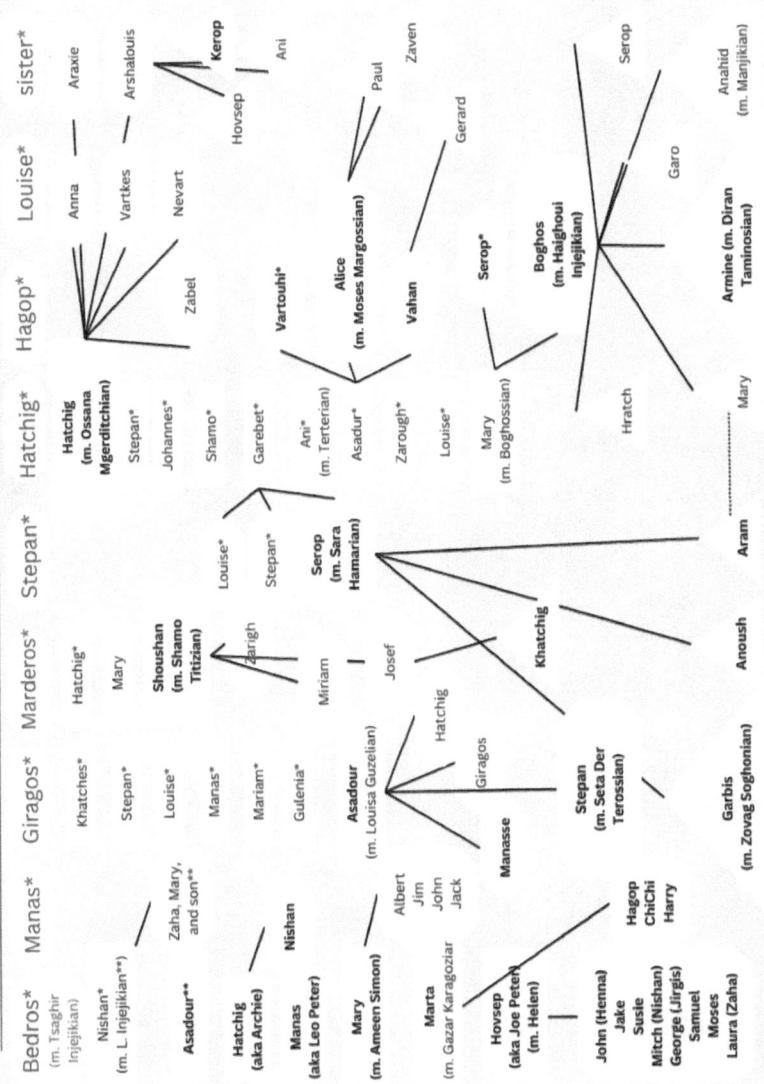

Karamardian family tree approx. 1890 – 1940

*indicates killed or deceased during 1915;

**indicates lost or stolen; names in bold indicates characters in book

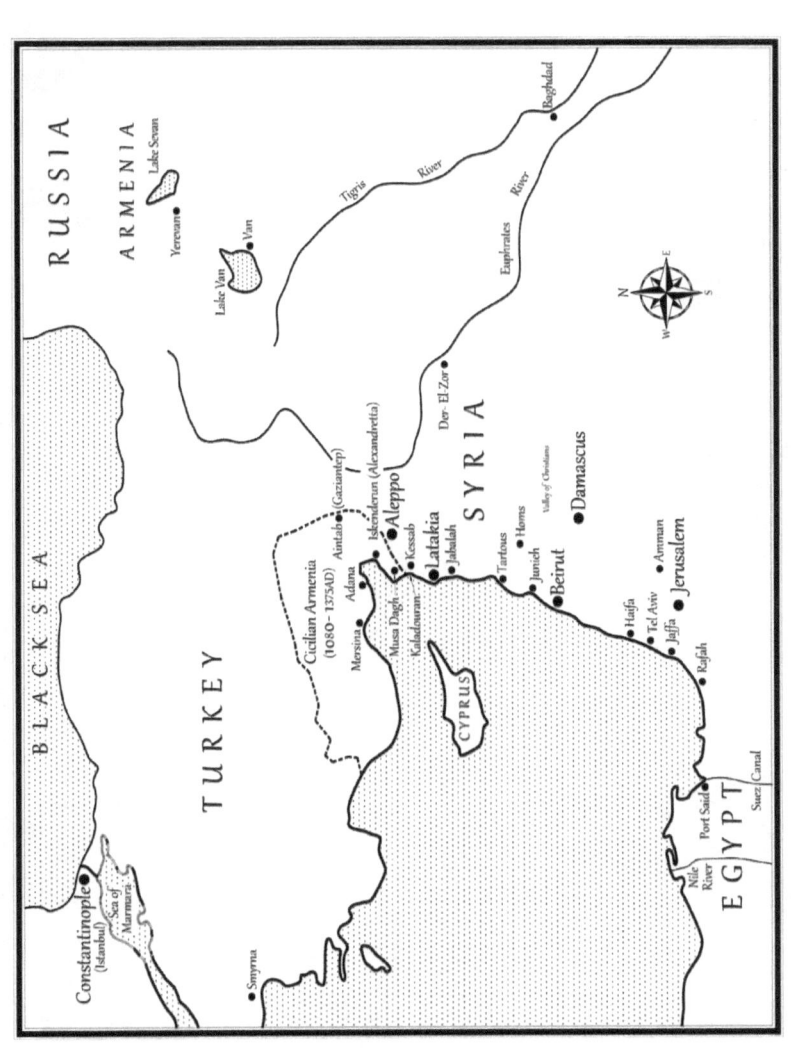

For Dad....

Publishing Services provided by Paper Raven Books LLC
Printed in the United States of America
First Printing, 2024

Cover image by Sossi Madzounian
Cover design by Kristin Designs

ISBN 979-8-9900982-0-6

TABLE OF CONTENTS

PROLOGUE

SYRIANS

AUTHOR

He swore at a Turk. At least, that's what they usually said. Sometimes, the story veered dramatically—that he had killed a Turk. They even seemed to enjoy the vagueness about it.

"Either way, Pa would have been hanged the next day, with a trial the day after!" Evidently, both crimes were punishable by death in the Ottoman Empire of 1904. I didn't know that part then, but I could recite this follow-up line by heart as soon as I could talk. It bellowed like the punchline to a favorite joke from whichever uncle was holding court at the moment.

Those few words, the byline of my grandfather's story, were never expanded on to offer the sort of detail such a statement ought to promise. But they were typical of a thousand anecdotes jockeyed about in jovial, yet earnest, argument between two or more uncles (and occasionally, an aunt) at any given time. I suppose they did not think of themselves as storytellers. There is a natural occurrence with any group of siblings finding themselves together in any one place at any one time; an inevitable instinct to compare notes, verify experiences; a validation of life's shared chapters, perhaps. Storytellers, nevertheless. Every single one!

They were poster children of the Great Depression, my six uncles and two aunts. The eight of them were, for a few years, augmented in number by an additional seven cousins—mostly male—and, in most summers, by even more cousins from Detroit, also mostly male! Though they woke, worked, and slept in the same house on the same farm in the same family, they might have lived on different continents. Each version of any given story depended on who was doing the telling, and who was refuting the details. The younger uncles argued more—and with less credibility.

Sam's voice was the loudest. "Jake hitched up the horses and let them run right into the tree line! That kid Teddy got his nose broke…"

When Uncle Moosey erupted in response, chortling so hard he choked on his own spit, there was no way Uncle Jake could let it pass.

"It wasn't his nose. It was his teeth! And I didn't let those damn horses run. They got spooked by a snake and took off. When we got to the tree, they split to either side of it!"

Mitch's tighter, less resonant tone managed to match Sam's volume. "They almost ran down me and George in the haying field, but we couldn't have stopped them. That pair was so wild Pa took those goddamn horses back to Old Doc Miller the very next day."

Over the roomful of bellowing laughter, Aunt Susie's gruff and gritty upstate twang, that years of living in Southern California would never tame, cut in. "You got it all wrong. We didn't even have that bad pair yet. Doc Miller's horses were okay… But Pa had to pay for that boy's teeth which I can tell you was a hefty bill. They never brought him round again either!"

George, my father, opened his mouth, but his intended words never landed since, even with a voice several decimals below the others, Uncle John spoke up. And, when the eldest of them spoke, his words took some magical sort of precedence. The younger uncles naturally deferred to him.

"Nah, that pair didn't come from Doc Miller at all. Pa won them in a poker game. No wonder they were defective as hell!" More laughter, resonant as the hollow caverns of dumbeks like the silver one perched on top of our living room organ.

Even youngest Aunt Laura might attempt to chime in but, drowned out in the din, her timid voice eventually trailed off and surrendered to the dominant boom of her brothers. This ritual preserved something for them, a bonding, perhaps. But the lively contradictions never ceased to humor and entertain the next generation—my siblings, cousins, and me. When their voices rose to dip into arguments over details of long-ago escapades, we automatically took note and tuned in. From our earliest ages, we stopped in the middle of our own games to inch closer and settle around them, spellbound.

Regardless of the version, once stories wended back to the subject of Jido, certain basics were established— etched in stone and never refuted. By all accounts, their "Pa" (my "Jido," pronounced *Jih' doh;* the word means grandfather in Arabic) had been spirited out of the country in the dead of night by his family, accompanied by a brother who did not arrive with him in New York, but was said to have ended up lost somewhere in South America. There was never variation on these facts. Nor were further details ever mentioned.

There were, however, other stories—mentions only—of murder, and sisters kidnapped by Turks and whisked away to harems. These teasers floated like opaque ghosts and joined the fairy tales in my head. The uncles' second-hand snippets of information about those stories were too limited to materialize into arguments. Those other stories lived in corners somewhere, at risk of fading away to dust. I suppose I always assumed that they would be revealed at some point. I think I had faith that such dramatic information would naturally come to light—maybe when I was older. Nobody ever elaborated beyond those comments, I thought, because they knew little about them. But everybody "knew" that Jido had left the "old country" in the middle of the night, with the lost brother. Until my twelfth year, it did not occur to me to ask why.

We were all together every Sunday and holiday, usually at either Uncle Sam's or our house, from sometime around noon until well beyond dark. The day would begin with clattering sounds of arrival: dishes being presented and commented on, coats offered and carried away. There, at the back door entrance where the corner wall was papered in green stencil-like murals of steamboats and willow trees, at least fifty voices poured into the small kitchen space. The most important moment was when Jido stepped through the door. As if a bell had rung, each and every one of us, parent and child alike, automatically approached to kiss him on both cheeks. He grinned into his dimples and said little, but he lit up the room. As far as I could tell, everything really began when he entered the house.

His snow-white hair had a very prominent streak of yellow running from the left temple to the crown of his head. It looked like the dye job of a Halloween prank but, in fact, was the stain of cigarette smoke constantly curling up and into his hair from the Lucky Strike that dangled between his two first fingers or rested in the ashtray next to his elbow on the card table. It was said he had smoked since he was seven!

To this day, a whiff of cigar smoke rocks me like a hot flash and catapults me to a typical Sunday scene with the extended family gathered in our little ranch house on Warren Road. The sweet cigar smell, mingled with fresh lemon and frying butter for pilaf, is accompanied by a symphony of sounds. From the living room, men's raucous laughter swells and subsides, certain swear words in Arabic (which we kids learned to recognize) punch out with the simultaneously slamming down of a card on the square, fold-out table. Only Jido and Uncle Jake stick to their Camels and Lucky Strikes while the others (except my dad) puff pungent cigar vapors into the surrounding atmosphere. From where the aunts cluster in the kitchen, the tinny chatter of their voices floats throughout the house, though often overpowered by a jubilant eruption from the card table. Secret whispers murmured by older girl cousins waft from my sister Patrice's bedroom, while from the basement, the unreserved squeals of childish games played by the younger cousins float upwards. I hear an engine start—my brother and older boy cousins, jammed into someone's car, managing to sneak out of the driveway before they are noticed.

The scene played out weekly, into my preteen years. In the center of the living room, perfectly situated in center frame of the requisite 50s ranch-style picture window, they sat around the card table playing pinochle—my uncles and Jido. (It was Always pinochle; Never poker!) The uncles' hair and eyes were as black as any I've seen; I was well aware of how they—we—stood out in crowds and restaurants, darker and more striking than average folk. Their heads surrounded Jido's white mane with its yellow streak. John, the eldest, was small and wiry. So, too, was the youngest, Moses, whom most called Moosey. He represented a tiny war hero, whose combat stories were whispered about among my boy cousins. He joked a lot and even teased me: ever since a punchline to one of his jokes had eluded me, he liked to call me *Density*. It made my face burn in embarrassment. Mitch was my personal hero because, well, he had horses, and I'd been horse crazy since I was nine! Jake, handsome as heck but with devilish eyes, was referred to as the "black sheep," which assured a mystery about him, though never fear. My father, George, was the only non-smoker in those years before smoking fell out of fashion in lieu of health concerns. (I always wondered how he managed to tolerate the surrounding cloud of pollution when, years later, with his sensitive nose and loathing of cigarette smoke, he would detect and bewail the smoke on my clothing after a night out.) Sam, the only tall uncle, towered above his brothers and, for some parties, donned a silk-patterned smoking jacket, invoking an ethnic version of the Rat Pack. Many a photograph captures him leading the debkee (line dancing), waving a white handkerchief and laughing jubilantly. More than any of them, he embodied the perfect example of post-war life enjoyed to the fullest in all its fervor and possibility.

The six of them were a motley extension of Jido. I thought of Jido on Sunday nights when my family watched the TV show "Bonanza," with Lorne Greene surrounded by his adoring sons. (Although the Bonanza brothers seemed more like my aunts' mild-mannered husbands—not a swear word slipping from either— lurking in the background of the vibrant, larger-than-life, Peter men.)

The uncles almost—but not quite—drowned out my grandfather's voice. Staccato Arabic words interlocked in bursts, often punctuated by an undoubtedly innovative phrase strung together with creative cuss words, were followed by unanimous laughter directed at whichever victim of the current hand of cards. Beaming faces, with those blackest of eyes, poked through the dense cloud of smoke. I cannot pull words from the recesses of memory because, frankly, I had never captured specific meaning from the sounds of their conversation and laughter. It took place in that guttural "Syrian" language reserved for their solidarity, their togetherness at the card table.

Yet I know for certain that it was joy I heard in those voices around the table, and Jido's happiness was a beacon emanating from the center. I felt it even though I did not understand the Arabic. Jido's voice had music in it, especially when he laughed, but it only now occurs to me that I didn't hear his words. He spoke so little, and only sparingly in English, that I never concerned myself with gleaning meaning from his few, clipped words. The uncles, however, hung on his every breath and move. I imagine now, how much they needed to absorb of him in those hours. They did not have access to him during the week like we did when he made the rounds visiting wives and grandkids, delivering his fresh baked loaves of Syrian bread.

He was the center of my universe when he was present. Wednesday morning was OUR day, when he arrived with the goods—what we called "Jido bread"—round and flat Syrian loaves that looked like pizza dough, golden and puffy—straight from his oven. Once he taught me to make the dough and cupped his hand to show me "*tis (this) much salt!*" When I poured salt into my small palm he grabbed my hand to study it and corrected himself, "*No, no, not your hand.... is more—TIS much salt!*" When he baked, he tossed the dough like pizzas and liked to see how close he could get it to our noses. I learned later that on other mornings he delivered the bounty to my cousins' homes. But on Wednesdays he was ours, and the bread always arrived hot. He must have piled it into the car in seconds flat and driven across town from his bungalow on South Hill.

The minute he pulled into the driveway we smelled the "Jido bread" and raced for the kitchen, anxious for his appearance at the back door. Mouths watering, we yanked off hunks like starving maniacs, lathered it with butter, rolled it up, and dipped our treasure into waiting mugs of hot cocoa. He wore a thin, short-sleeved white shirt—the flimsy, lightweight kind of the tropics—no tie, and loose trousers of either grey or greenish color. He lost no time digging into the baggy pockets, where he carried yellow packs of Juicy Fruit gum, and tossed a pack to each of us, expecting us to catch it. And he laughed at us groveling on the floor to scoop it up.

I loved the times that he played with us, undistracted by his grown-up sons, and chuckled and teased us mercilessly. But I hated when he leaned over the couch and held me captive on my back for the "tickle." I despised being tickled. I kicked helplessly and screamed upwards at his dimpled chin and twinkling eyes while he laughed deep and long. I don't know if my sisters experienced the same fate or if it was only my dramatic reaction that made the effort to torture me so worthwhile. An Alpha Male would continue tickling through my sobs with a self-confidence that bordered on cruelty. But Jido was not cruel. Even then, I believed with certainty that he mistook my squeaks and gasps for laughter while I, breathless and teary, could not express myself beyond the ambiguous helplessness of a faint and weepy "stop! Help!" I both loved the attention and suffered the method of receiving it.

On Christmas Day, without fail, there would be an envelope on the tree for each of twenty-seven grandkids, containing a fortune—a five-dollar bill! Aunt Ruth disclosed to me years later that it was she who wrote out our names on all those envelopes every year. Jido could not write in English. But he could speak, it seemed to me, in any language!

In 1960, we moved for several years to Puerto Rico for the ground breaking of the Arecibo Observatory, the focus of my father's career. I was just seven when we arrived, one of only three American families in our new community. In our second year there, Jido came to stay awhile. When he waltzed into the house, he seemed as natural and native as our Puerto Rican neighbors. He teased and giggled with the teenaged maid Elena. She, herself, was no timid child, having marched into my parents' bedroom early one Saturday morning to inform them she was going to work for them, and proceeded to insert herself into our lives, no matter how anyone felt about it. The two of them—my grandfather and Elena—chattered incessantly in Spanish.

"*Vai comier, Viejo!*" She called him "old man."

"*No hai importancia, muchacha!*" He doled out equal insults to the "little girl."

He played jokes on her. The best one was when Jido chased Elena up onto the roof. (We often played on our flat roof and the ladder remained propped in place). She hesitated and looked back, expecting him to follow. Instead, laughing uproariously, he pulled away the ladder, leaving her stranded, screaming and cursing words I didn't recognize. Neighbors came out to see what the ruckus was and joined the hilarity, seeming to cheer Jido as streams of Spanish words also poured from his lips, like a native! My parents had struggled through night classes and could barely utter anything. We kids fared better, through school and playing with neighbor kids, but not with the effortless ease of Jido's Spanish. I had no idea then that his life in America had begun right there in the Caribbean islands, in Spanish! Someone said that he spoke Turkish, too, and who knew what else? Here's what I thought: if he could speak any language, he could do anything; therefore, maybe so could I. I just knew it was magic. Jido was magic, pure and simple. So, it was obvious (to me) that I came from a magical family.

For the first twelve years of my life, the essence of Jido dominated my world. I assumed he was the center of my parents' world, too—it made perfect sense—and that of my many uncles, aunts, siblings, and cousins. We went to Syrian festivals called hufflas with an extended family group and the Syrian community. An Arabic band came from Utica and joined Jido's friend, Eliah Baida, who played oud and sang haunting Syrian melodies. Food and tents were set up around the little church perched on Syrian Hill above the old salt block at Myers Park, a little ways up the north shore of Cayuga Lake. We danced, stamping our feet and hopping in a line dance, called the debkee, led by Uncle Sam and others waving handkerchiefs. This dance was fun because everyone could do it, from five-year-olds to the oldest men and women, but the day's highlight was the featured belly dancing. We formed a natural circle, clapping hands and oohing at the dancer, and I idolized the floating silks and weaving arms above a body that arched backward. All around me, accented voices of the old people filled the air with Syrian words.

There were other extended family around too. Second cousins that we didn't see every week, like the Mikes. Everyone's last name was *Mike, George, Abraham,*

John, Solomon, Isaac, etc. It made sense to me, therefore, that ours was *Peter.* This was our clan and the identity felt natural in a town of Italian, Greek, Irish, and Jewish friends. We were called the 'camel riders.' My older siblings were sometimes called by a nickname of Camel or Pete by their peers. Most of our homes sported a camel saddle, featured on one side of the fireplace like a stool (the other side usually sported a television set). We proudly adored Danny Thomas and Paul Anka as countrymen, the way our Italian friends claimed Frank Sinatra and Dean Martin.

The aunts and uncles not only spun tales of the farm where they appeared to raise hell, but also what they thought they knew of the "old country:" scenes that had been delivered to them in full drama by Sito, my late grandmother, around the stove in the years before they acquired a radio for entertainment. She was the source of all their knowledge—Jido said little to nothing, it seems—and they shared highlights spun from her stories.

"She took one look at Pa at the salt block and thought, 'That's the man I'm gonna marry!'" said Uncle John. "But the men of her village forbade it. Pa had to fight 'em all, one at a time."

"She carried bags of salt, on all four feet ten inches of her," said Dad. We were far from Syria and all the stories felt as far away as fairy tales can, but I was aware that I was part of something larger than my skinny pre-teen self. I never knew Sito, who died when I was six months old, but Jido was everything. And enough for me.

The night Dad told us, I sat on my bed, stunned, the word 'gone' spinning round my head, clutching wildly for its meaning. It was my first encounter with death, a new and foreign idea that I was unprepared to consider. I was unaware that Jido had lingered or languished. Sure, I recall when we went to the new hospital up along the west side overlooking the lake. That may have been my first time in a hospital. We had to wait our turns entering the room and there lay Jido, it was just Jido! He smiled and joked. Like normal. Like the next day, the next time…

Jido-less space was incomprehensible.

The funeral imprinted itself in my adolescent DNA. It began at the cavernous Presbyterian Church that Jido belonged to, and which dwarfed our smaller Baptist church next door. I sat in the third row with siblings and cousins. A rocking sound like thunder began, then a tremor, the floor seemed to shake. The pews in front of us were creaking, rocking unevenly, scraping against the floor so hard from the bodies—racked with sobbing—of Dad and the uncles, I held my breath, frightened the wood would crack and my family would tumble out into the aisle. Then we were outside where a never-ending parade of cars lined up along the street. A stranger in black counted off three to four grandkids at a time and directed us into each car. When we arrived at King Cemetery at the top of the hill, I turned and looked out the back window, freeze-framing a scene that has never left me. A line of cars behind us snaked down Quarry Hill Road and through town, all the way to the church. I thought then, for the very first time, about the number of people—other people—who must have loved my grandfather. It stunned me. In that moment, I realized that he had belonged to many more than "us." Who was he to all these people? I wondered then. I wonder if I'll ever stop asking the question.

The weekend of the funeral stretched into several days of family gathering at Uncle Sam's. It was then that my world forever shifted. Because I was doomed to have been born in a substantial age crack between my many cousins who congregated according to age groups, I was often banned from the big girls' company and hung out with my aunts. On this night the aunts included me in the card game they had set up around the kitchen table and were teaching me to play poker. This felt rebellious, because the menfolk never played poker in our house.

We were all giggling when one of them, Aunt Ruth, casually said, "You know, Jido was actually not Syrian. He was Armenian." I froze in place, the ground below me shuffling, changing shape—was this an earthquake or my imagination—silently seeking words for the obvious question screaming in my head:

What is Armenian? But I was unable to muster a sound as Aunt Ruth continued,

"And, you know, all his family were killed by Turks. But he never, *ever* talked about it…"

CHAPTER 1

OLD COUNTRY

Kaladouran, Kessab, Syria - 1896

HOVSEP

The beach in Kaladouran formed a perfect crescent, just like the skinny moon lurking above the steep mountain that backed up against it in a dark embrace—almost menacing, to someone not accustomed to its presence. Lapping waves, drowned out by the sharp winds that swirled and bounced and whooped against the cliffs, sounded more like a dog's panting than any substantive statement by the sea. The shadows now descended on the cliffs in that certain angle that told Hovsep it was time to climb the path back up to the house. He imagined he could smell chunks of lamb that must be simmering in pots of loobi stew with green beans and tomatoes, and soon to be ladled over pilaf. Or, possibly the lamb he was smelling was ground up with onions and peppers and spread atop baking lamajoun meat pies, surely ready to exit the ovens on both sides of the shared family gardens housing today's feast.

His eyes caught the flash of a white shirt sleeve flapping on a cluster of jutting boulders a few meters away. He stepped barefoot over the ragged edges to swoop it up and dress himself. His shirt, vest, and shoes were all that remained on the shore after the refreshing summer dip he and his brothers had stolen between the wedding ceremony and feast. Asadour often initiated such impulsive side adventures, but it was rare for Nishan to be persuaded along with the scheme. He was already twelve, almost a man, and very serious about that.

"Do you honestly suppose anybody will notice our wet hair, when they all are sure to be drenched from the climb up from the church?" Asadour teased, as was his nature. He had been the first to strip and, together in what seemed like the same moment, splash into a wave—also his nature.

Nishan followed, but so carefully that even Hovsep laughed at the manner at which he folded his trousers and shirt before laying them gently on a separate boulder, as if his own clothes might be tarnished by the haphazard manner in which Asadour's garments lay crumpled, should they touch. But Hovsep forced a kinder voice, out of respect for his elder brother.

"They won't even know we slipped away. Enjoy the swim, Nishan!"

How they had giggled like girls at the waves that assaulted them, and also for the fact that they had somehow pulled off a disappearance coup. Hovsep now looked down at the stones where all their wedding costumes had lain a short time ago. How long had he lingered here?

The fact that his brothers were nowhere to be seen further confirmed the hour. The wedding feast must be close to ready, presented on the long planks placed across piles of boulders and draped with embroidered linens, under the shade of trellised grapevines. Family and villagers would be congregating with relief after a long, drawn-out stroll uphill from the ceremony at the church—such a long interim that Hovsep, Nishan, and Asadour had plenty of time to run down to the beach and cool off. His brothers had not lingered like he. Whatever thoughts had distracted him from the festivities above now vanished, and Hovsep turned to scramble up the rocky incline that levelled off at two adjacent Karamardian homes.

The homestead overlooked the beach from its perch higher up the valley. It was connected to Uncle Giragos' house by a sprawling four and a half acres of garden, which offered much more growing space than the other uncles' homes, four kilometers away in the town center of Kessab. Uncle Giragos shared the groves and garden patches, where drying figs and apricots were slung from the grapevines and bougainvilleas were distributed throughout, punctuating the plots of produce—tomatoes, koussa (squash), babagnoush (eggplant), and okra. Like everyone in his family, regardless of age or gender, Hovsep adored the garden, whether working it or enjoying it at leisure. Between the houses, brothers and cousins constantly raced back and forth through the vineyard paths, both in play and work tasks.

Many in the family shared more than property—they shared names, such as Hovsep's brother Asadour—Asadour of Bedros, and his little cousin Asadour—Asadour of Giragos, born with the same surname of Karamardian. There were many cousin Khatchigs and Marys, for example. But nobody in Kessab appeared to struggle with the commonality of names. Besides the identifying factor of fathers, there was a tradition of nicknames. It was just as common for them to be all together on Sundays, when the entire Karamardian clan flocked to the beach; family units from town spent much of the summer sharing Kaladouran meals cooked mostly over the shishkabob pit in Bedros' and Giragos' gardens and would walk the few miles back to Kessab center under the stars.

Today marked the final day of Shoushan's wedding festivities. Hovsep's pretty cousin had married village neighbor Shamo Titizian at the Evangelical Church that had been built by Presbyterian missionaries many years ago. Hovsep's many uncles and aunties were milling about. Nishan and Asadour were already lurking near the table, anxiously awaiting the summons to eat, and Hovsep spotted his little brother Khatchig and their cousin Asadour toddling among legs and long swishy skirts. The new baby, Manas, was not in his mother's arms, nor on the hip of an aunt—likely tucked away asleep in the house, Hovsep thought. There were plenty of Injejikians, too—Mayrig's sisters Julie and Teshkoun, and many cousins from his mother's side. The smell of laurel trees pervaded the air, but fell short of overpowering the aromas from the ovens.

When Hovsep breathlessly arrived at the scene— this tribe of his people with their sound alike names—he stopped short for a brief moment and stared, unaware exactly why, yet overcome with a wild desire to take in the sight of his family closing in and milling about the tables and roasting pit. The Kessabtsi dialect undulated with currents of breeze, alternating between clipped final consonants and soothing opening ones, like the shushing of a baby. It presented the sort of reflection one might expect from an older man experiencing a scene that comes less and less often, rather than the momentary insight of an eight-year-old. But it gradually occurred to young Hovsep that this scene was about to become a seasonal, less frequent occurrence, and he expelled a sigh of understanding that was rather astute, and odd, for a mere boy to emit.

They would come home for summers, of course, after the move. He would again enjoy the consistency of summer home meals with most of the family on those long stretches of unstructured days without school demands. He took this for granted from somewhere deep inside. But he was most aware that of all his regrets from the move, he would miss his Kessab school. Wow! He could hardly believe he just said that to himself. Wasn't he the most impatient boy at the school? So said the missionary teacher and even his cousins. He tried to imagine not hearing the Kessabtsi language on a daily basis. He was not yet well versed in Arabic, and that was going to have to be reckoned with in the new school at the Mission in the old city of Ladehkiya. What would it feel like—being "*odar*?" Mostly he would miss this overflowing group of guardians—these people of his flesh, his language, his blood, his dreams—laughing together or pulling him aside with words of guidance. Or maybe just setting up pranks and waiting expectantly with glowing eyes for the inevitable reaction. A few of his uncles were real pranksters, though most were solemn, like his elderly father. At eight-years-old, Hovsep could not be expected to understand how sheltered his life was.

"Ai, Hovsep! There you are! Get over here, boy, before your plate is claimed by a ghost!" Aunt Kitchka clapped his back as he grabbed a plate. Forks clanged against the metal outdoor bowls, voices ebbed and flowed, and girl cousins bustled about removing and replacing platters.

After supper the family clustered in groups; the men dragged stools to a spot on the slope, formed a ring beneath the fullest laurel tree, and lit pipes or cigarettes. A grove of trees in the vicinity—mostly pomegranate, orange, and apple—distributed that combination of sweet and pungent aromas that continually whet the appetite. The uncles distributed apples and oranges which they held in one hand, while slicing chunks of the fruit to stick in their mouths directly from a knife in the other hand; this was a customary habit for digestion and also camaraderie. Occasionally, a pomegranate was halved and its seeds scooped with the knife, men chuckled at the inevitable clumsiness of dropped seeds. Hovsep loved to eavesdrop while pretending to kick a can around. Sometimes the echo of the can hitting a trunk or stone drowned out a whole sentence that he regretted missing. But this time he was concerned and careful. Nishan was sitting with the men too, so he would be able to compare notes at bedtime.

"The location is good, on the edge between two quarters so you'll have both Armenian and Arab customers. Everybody buys the Yemeni! And the leather market is just nearby; for you no more weekly trudging to the market from Kessab for supplies!" Uncle Giragos was very encouraging about Father's new shoe shop in the city. "In fact, when I come to market in Ladehkiya, I will have a place to rest and break the trip into two parts."

"Of course you will, and you will sleep until morning for a fresh drive," Bedros assured him. Uncle Hagop, who lived in the city already, was expanding his shoe shop to join with Bedros. He had already secured a home for his brother's growing family of five boys and counting.

"And the house is a good one, with a garden! Tzaghir will like it," he countered. Murmurs and nods around the group.

Hovsep involuntarily clenched at the next comment, an afterthought by Hayrig (Father). "Of course, the boys must learn Arabic for school. As *odar*, it will be an adjustment."

"Ah, but they are young and resilient! It will be good for them. And Nishan will be apprenticing with us by year's end anyway," Hagop offered. "Bedros," he added softly, "the missionaries will look out for them, as always."

Marderos called for his daughter Shoushan, as was custom for a new bride, to serve coffee. This prompted Bedros to repeat the order to his wife—after all, he was the host—and the conversation abruptly shifted to other matters. Hovsep reluctantly went to look for a cousin or brother, in hope of temporary distraction until the day's end.

The lowering sun over the far end of the Mediterranean was the highlight of each day in Kaladouran; it paced a slow descent from the other side of the world over the sliver of beach that was too narrow for the gigantic family to picnic on. Besides, the view at day's end was even more satisfying from the gardens above, regardless of weather. As the night's blackness engulfed the village, the family's awe only increased when a billion blinking stars began to fill up the deepening purple sky and illuminate the valley so narrow, it was less than a half mile wide. Sometimes, if cloud cover hid the stars, Hovsep felt swallowed up and the darkness suffocated. But most nights the deep, bottomless spectacle of light against dark lit his soul with magic. The sounds of his family, the "oohs and ahs," intensified his enjoyment at nightfall in Kaladouran. His simple needs were also fulfilled during these summer days of tending to garden vegetables, a chore he did not at all mind, or wandering the steep paths of the mountain they called Celderan with his friend Vahan, or brother Asadour. And when they walked the four kilometers to the town center of Kessab, there was plenty to occupy young minds and muscles.

All that summer of 1896 the mornings were glorious, but Mayrig was heavy in her pregnancy. The morning after Shoushan's wedding, Nishan went with Hayrig and Uncle Hagop to the city to oversee some arrangements for the new home. Hovsep helped his mother with packing. Usually Mayrig sang tunes while she cooked and Hovsep felt, when he lingered near, as if the melodies unraveling from her throat were invented just for him. He imagined himself alone in those moments with her—just mother, son, and song—and filled up inside with a sort of invincibility—a knowing that harm would not reach them. Now, however, her lips were pressed together, silent. She smiled occasionally but her face was wan with fatigue, and Hovsep ached for her burden of extra chores for moving so close to her time.

"Mayrig, please do not lift the basket. Let me do the picking up of each one after you fill it... please!"

He felt important at his age, able to help his mother and at the same time anxious for the baby to come out and relieve her of the heavy load. He had been unaware of such things when Khatchig and, just last year, Manas were born, but now he was older and capable of so much. Still, once they had completed a good amount of folding fabrics and filling baskets, he was relieved when she retired for a rest, and Hovsep could slip away to look for his friend Vahan and perhaps walk the mountainside where they would always find something to kick around or explore on the slopes and beach.

Vahan was still in the village; his family stayed at his uncle's home and would not return to Kessab until later in the week. Including Kaladouran, five villages surrounded Kessab, the center town sprawled among the foothills six miles from the sea, with its colorfully tiled clay roofs that repelled water. Many Kessab families kept summer homes in the villages. But Uncle Giragos and Hovsep's father and mother lived year-round in Kaladouran, a canyon between two mountains that stretched steeply from the sea to Celderan Mountain. No matter, Bedros was moving his tribe away. The olive trees were no longer producing much, and the olive industry was unsustainable for the size the family had become. The family business of new shoes was a side trade for some of them, but for Bedros it would now become the mainstay of his income, as it was already for most of his brothers.

Hovsep's leisure time with friends was winding down and there was not a moment to lose. He had been to Ladekiya before the move, of course. On occasions the family had loaded up the cart and attended festivals, visiting Uncle Hagop and others in the Armenian Quarter. The thought of not being in Kessab until next summer was so depressing that Hovsep cast the subject out of his head as he raced to look for Vahan. In a week's time, life was going to change. He knew it was going to be different but could not yet comprehend in what ways. He was a young boy in a town of Armenians. Before too long—just a few years—he would be a teenager in a city of Arabs where there were rules, many rules that had yet to present themselves. But he did not know this today. After saying goodnight to Vahan, he kicked some stones all the way home. By the time he reached his family's house, the home Hayrig had just yesterday arranged the sale of to the Merserlian family, Mayrig was awake and preparing dinner over the stone oven that took up a whole wall in the kitchen.

He hoped that by joining her in the big cooking room, she would be in the mood and feeling well enough to share stories. He counted on these moments as much as he expected meals to sustain him. Father was silent most of his waking days, even among the uncles and the public. He simply was not a man of words. Were it not for Mayrig, the boys would know little of their hometown, their family, their heritage, even of their oppressors. Her stories or account of events in family life often held some sort of extra meaning or warning that was never overtly expressed but tucked inside the tale like an ivory mini doll that one finds upon biting into a sweet cake. Hovsep waited expectantly for her words, but instead she asked him to fetch some laurel (bay) leaves and zatah. He obediently slipped through the door at the end of the wall that opened directly into the first section of the gardens, neatly tended into patches of herbs. More than anything else, he would miss these gardens of Kaladouran.

CHAPTER 2

CITY OF LOSS

Latakia - 1901

HOVSEP

Nishan was already working in the shoe shop with Father and Uncle Hagop, molding the red leather Yemeni shoes to various sizes. There was even talk about finding him a wife, but that would wait a few months more, until after the new baby was born. Mayrig was again due and she was doing poorly, unable to stand and cook, feet swollen, and fatigued when she tried to sit up. The littlest Mary had only just begun school but for now was kept home. Aunt Julie had come to help. The boys, too, sulked near home on this day that was swelling with a nervous current, while the family collectively held its breath.

The night was interminable, the longest of Hovsep's life to date. Mayrig was surrounded by three women from the Armenian quarter, plus her two sisters from Kessab. Mary was sent to the outside stove to keep water boiling and banged the pots about while cries pierced the household. The boys hid in the garden, every last one of them except Nishan, who sat with Father and the Injejikian uncles in the parlour. Hovsep could smell fear in his brothers before his stomach lurched with the recognition of his own. He imagined that they would not be creeping into the long, narrow boys' room to sleep that night. Eventually they even huddled together—he could not recall ever doing this before—clutching each other, knowing. Something was far from normal and maybe very wrong. By morning it was over. Over in every way.

There was no more Mayrig.

The Baby Marta cried for her mother all the next day, desperately hungry for the body that had first sustained but then, rejected her. Hovsep tenderly longed to comfort her but didn't have a clue what to do. Aunt Julia rocked and soothed and tried to get her to suck goat milk from a cloth. Mary moved around the house with an immobile face. little Hovsep suspected that she could not dare let one face muscle adjust or she would dissolve. Asadour had no such compunction: he sobbed openly, constantly, resoundingly. Khatchig and Manas gritted their teeth in silence and avoided the house, finding chores or errands to do all day long.

Nishan and Father stoically went about the motions of arrangements. It was the only conversation heard in the house that day beyond an aunt's whisper to eat or a comforting shush to baby Marta. There was a burial to tend to, and it must be in Kessab. His mayrig— Tzaghir Injejikian Karamardian, nickname Haigha— would go home to Kaladouran where the Injejikian and Karamardian families shared resting spots in the village cemetery. Once there, Hovsep, helpless, found himself mindlessly drawn to the old garden between Uncle Giragos' home and his childhood house, now belonging to the Merserlians. He yanked weeds with a vengeance, dug holes needlessly, and wondered if he might one day ache less, know less, and therefore, hurt less. He knew he could not change a thing, only hope to stop caring, at least enough to go on.

The cemetery was high up the gorge. Hovsep could not believe how the ocean that stretched beyond them on the cliff glistened and twinkled so in the sunlight. How dare it mock his family, gathered at this solemn affair, as if it were any other day! He barely registered the women's wailing as he stared at the grave, buried in his wretchedness. When the group moved away, he knew his feet were moving, and when the family ate standing up holding plates while clustered in softly murmuring groups, he may have nibbled a bite of bread or lamb. But he did not know of any words he spoke or that were spoken to him; he did not know what his brothers were doing. He could not recall any one specific aunt or uncle, not even his father, in his memory afterwards. Nor did he try to. He floated through the worst day of his life and blocked it out thereafter.

When they returned from the funeral in Kessab, and burial at Kaladouran, the house suffocated him. He spent more and more time wandering the streets when not in school. He worked the gardens and showed Mary how to bake bread the way Mayrig had taught him. When school finished, he would be expected to enter the family shoe business like Nishan. The day would come all too soon, four years only, when his school days would end. He considered that he should be ecstatic in anticipation but somehow the vision of the shoe shop in the dusty quarter—the dim rooms inside, far from gardens or sunlight—filling with Syrians who stomped through the doorways and demanded service, treating his father, uncle, and brother as servants—planted in him a dread that spread through his body like a toxin.

CHAPTER 3

EZ

Latakia - 1904

HOVSEP

School wasn't so bad after all. Khatchig, three years behind him, had a calm disposition and managed without incident, though Manas hated it and suffered greatly at the hands of some Arab boys. Asadour had, for a while, suffered even more, but he seemed to have finally created a personal space for himself and a way not to be bothered. Asadour had a soft facial expression, his words and gestures were gentle. Sometimes he would wander aimlessly and observe the comings and goings of the city from his own sort of world, taking them in as if they were part of the books he read, even jotting down notes. Often, he would be beaten by two boys at a time and would just pick himself up and wordlessly walk to a corner, squat or sit and open his notebook.

It was as if he amazingly did not experience pain or humiliation. Hovsep suspected that he must have felt something, though Asadour could remove himself from his body and rob the boys of their glory with his passive absence of reaction. Hovsep chuckled at his brother's cleverness, but he himself never tolerated such insult. He fought off any boy who touched him with neat, clean counter punches, and attacks against his own person had long ago ceased.

His pity was all for Manas. It seemed his young, slight brother was bearing the brunt of bored Syrians who ran out of Armenians to terrorize. The missionaries would sometimes break up the fights, and they would cease for a bit, but Manas tried to overcome his smallness by taunting and tempting too much and would eventually pay the price. Hovsep and Asadour were now teenagers and beyond these concerns. They had new rules to worry about.

Naturally, the boys and girls at the mission school were Christian. But the world outside the school was run by Turks. Ottomons, the *effendis* liked to call themselves. Now that the two brothers were past the "certain" age of twelve, they were required to wear a stupid fez on their heads in public; the conical Ottomon hat made Hovsep's anger surge—especially the sight of it on his father's head. It was typical of Turks to press upon the Armenians their own customs and dress, as if his people were inferior and not allowed to be themselves. Bullies, every one of them! And Syrian Muslims were their lap dogs, scurrying behind them to lick their very… Hovsep swallowed and decided not to think about the Turkish authorities whose brutality was random, sudden, and inexplicable whenever it descended. Christian Syrians had it hardly better with the Turks, so there was at least solidarity with many of his classmates at the mission school, even friendships among them.

Manas had befriended a much younger friend at school, the little American boy named Walter. The headmaster sometimes placed Walter, along with Manas, under Hovsep's supervision—much to Manas' indignation and Hovsep's annoyance. Yet, Walter was interesting for a little child and told the brothers about things he knew from another place his family had lived. His grandfather had started the mission schools in all of Turkey, many years before. The Ladehkiya mission was a temporary assignment for Walter's father, but they had been in Syria for many years and Walter had known no other home as yet. They came from Amirka, the one where they speak English, and not the Spanish-speaking one where most of the Kessabtsi boys who leave emigrate to. Walter spoke halting Arabic, even a few words in Armenian, and they traded language phrases for fun, like a card game. The children in school studied French, as required, and sometimes a little English from certain missionary teachers, though Hovsep found it an impossible language. Walter asked his mother for the English versions of the brothers' names and delightfully used these as nicknames for his friends: he called Hovsep "*Josef*" and Manas "*Leo*." He had no nicknames for Asadour or Khatchig. Hovsep was okay with it; it sounded like the Arabic version of his name, Youssef, so he was able to recognize and respond. Manas found his nickname too funny to repeat. Behind Walter's back they snickered at what they considered the funniest name of all—*Walter*!

The mission school in the city was much larger than the one at Kessab, a maze of complex rooms and gardens, and any boys with Walter had free rein of it, whooping and giggling as they raced through corridors with no one to hear or be bothered. At times, Walter came to the house, and Hovsep had a feeling that Walter might have more interest in his sister Mary than in a friendship with the bullish Manas. He clearly relished the Karamardian household and garden and Mary's cooking, which differed slightly from the meals cooked by Syrian women in the mission kitchens. Besides, everyone who came through the Bedros Karamardian household was astonished to taste meals mostly prepared by a nine-year-old child! Hovsep imagined Mary humored little Walter with a motherly attention and, quite naturally, in total innocence of his crush. Nothing could ever have come of it, friendship or romance, even if she were not Walter's senior by a year or two. She would be married to an Armenian, of course, at the proper time. Yet unlike other Armenian girls, Mary had not benefited from school. Since Mayrig had died, she took on the care of baby Marta and, gradually, the rest of the household. Hovsep wondered if she missed the attention of the missionaries that other girls at school seemed to enjoy. In Syria, only Armenians sent their girls to attend school. And all Armenian girls seemed to want to go. Mary pretended she didn't care. Nor did he dare to ask her and be rebuffed in front of Hayrig.

Mary's red hair was not unique but nor was it common, and she was considered pretty by everyone, friend and family alike, anytime the topic of women was discussed. Bedros was said to have red hair, too, but Hovsep could not recall his father's hair other than a light grey. The boys were all dark-haired, though Khatchig and Asadour had light eyes like Mary and some other Armenians. Nishan and Asadour had some problems with their eyes, like Father. In each of their faces, one of the eyes seemed to float towards the other when both were looking straight ahead. And one time, he thought he noticed the same in little Marta's eyes.

As the final days of his school life approached, Hovsep felt anxiety creep into his bones. He had managed to hold it at bay the entire year, even spending less time with Asadour, who finished up the previous year. Brother Asadour had been spared the family trade. The missionaries saw in him a potential for teaching; he enjoyed the classics and was already apprenticing with dominion over the youngest grades in reading. Asadour seemed to master Arabic, even penning an occasional poem, which Hovsep had little interest in reading. The two gravitated toward individual interests in the precious spare time between school and chores. Hovsep liked to garden, tinker, fix broken wagons, and do anything that was outside and airy. He truly enjoyed wandering the old Armenian quarter, its maze of shops and small huts that had been built to house crusaders sheltered by the Armenian population over five hundred years before. Asadour, who once gladly partnered these explorations, now declined in favor of a book.

The Karamardian shoemakers of Ladehkiya had begun discussing another expansion, since Khatchig and even Manas would also finish school in a few years' time. Hovsep could not help but sense the trap looming ahead. On the last day of classes and therefore, this seventeen-year-old's perceived freedom, Hovsep wandered aimlessly on the way to the market to buy some fabric at Mary's request. She wished to make a dress for Marta, who was four now and more visible to the public and in need of proper clothing. He would begin his apprenticeship in the shop the following day and was grateful for the distraction of the task and a final opportunity to wander the Armenian quarter.

Rounding the corner to the city square that held hundreds of cramped stalls, he suddenly realized with alarm that he had forgotten the requisite fez on his head. Too late, he was spotted by a group of gendarmes who moved toward him. He tried to think fast: he could run. He could apologize. But before he had sifted through the options, he heard one of the "turds" yelling something—a 'dirty Armenian dog' the first audible phrase, followed by worse. Hovsep's head exploded. He felt hands grab at him, his body tensed—a coil winding up, then springing back—the next moment blurred. Hovsep's only clear memory for the remainder of his life would be of the running that followed—running for his life—and of voices shouted, louder and louder, closer and closer to home…

Someone was running down the street, calling, "Mary, Khatchig! Get your father!"

Hiding… Breathing in gulps, heart pounding… A voice whispered, "Stay there! Let the grapevines cover you until dark…"

When the boat finally pulled off from the dock, Hovsep could not work out how many hours had passed—it

had been dark for a very long time—but he thought
he might risk a breath at last. How long had he been
unconsciously holding the air in his lungs? So sudden.
What happened to him? He was leaving his home with
no thought prior to this moment, no planning or preparation; whatever this is… he shuddered… was only
hours in the making. Someone had raced to the shop to
warn his father. Someone had hidden him in a neighbor's
garden. Uncle Hagop and Father pulled together all their
contacts and secured a ship leaving before dawn. He had
not said goodbye to Manas, Khatchig, or little Marta,
who would be heartbroken. She was not even five and
would forget all about him–oh, what has happened?

He tried to focus on what he did know, anything
that could slow his heart rate. He knew that the ship
would dock at Ishkenderan by noon, and they would
have to book passage on a transport with many ports
of call—names he had studied in school printed on
maps of the Mediterranean Sea. The ideal destination
would be Marseille, France. After that, there would
be ships going west somewhere and somehow—they
would have to see what's what. His nose caught a whiff
of something. Across his shoulder was slung a hastily
wrapped meal for two—probably bread and dolma and
some of the smelly shankleesh cheese his sister Mary
had made only that day, its pungent odor permeating
the canvas pouch. She had shoved the package into his

arms as they fled the house. In his pocket he felt coins to pay for another passage. Asadour had some too.

Asadour! He suddenly remembered. Asadour was with him! Thank God for Brother Asadour, already sleeping in the bunk, who saw an opportunity and wanted desperately to accompany him to the unknown. Mind jumping to Hayrig, Hovsep felt his breath go shallow once more, his stomach clenched in a new way. His father had only briefly embraced him in brisk farewell—it was not his way to be overly tender—and had uttered just five words: "Take care of your brother."

He had likely said the very same thing to Asadour. Hayrig could not have wanted Asadour to go and yet knew that with two of them, their chances improved against theft and deceit. It hardly seemed fair that Father could lose two sons at once. Hovsep took another sharp breath and commanded himself not to think. He tried to ground his mind in the present and avoid the bottomless depth of wishful thinking, a practice that would serve him well in the future.

Behind him, the marina built upon columns of ancient civilizations stretched endlessly in a welcoming gesture like open arms to the port city of Ladehkiya. He glanced over his shoulder at the night, still a blend of darkness punctuated with the twinkling lights of various lamps scattered haphazardly from the end of the pier throughout the streets. Fully wrapped in a surrounding cloak of agriculture—cotton and tobacco—the city sat fifty-nine kilometers south from the border town of Kessab, Hovsep's true family home and summer haven. Hovsep allowed his mind a moment to hover up the coastline and imagine the beach at Kaladouran, then turn back to the city behind him where, deep in its center, on the edge of the Armenian quarter, stood the Karamardian shoe shop.

Helplessly, Hovsep surrendered to thoughts of Father and Uncle Hagop, who would be at work soon. Perhaps they would open early to shake off the tension of the preceding twelve hours, pick up trimmed soles to attach to the red leather of future shoes, maybe sigh a deep breath of relief from the close call. Perhaps Uncles Giragos and Shamo would visit this week; they often brought a cart from Kessab for shoe supplies and stayed for the night at Bedros' home, breakfast provided by little Mary, before hitting the morning leather market and the full day trip home. Deep into the night they might talk with Hayrig, thought Hovsep, become informed of the latest developments, and mourn the loss of two nephews, speculating and praying for their safe journey. Hovsep allowed himself just one last moment to wish his own presence at the shop, safely running his hands over a length of red leather, oblivious to danger.

The sea lapped the sides of the boat as it picked up speed, and Hovsep turned his face back into the wind. Do not look back at the harbor lights receding behind. He would no longer be able to hold his tears. No use. He felt water on his cheeks. Could it be the wind meeting the waves and throwing splashes at his face? Do not look back. From now on it is all ahead. He would make a new life. If it was a good life, he would send for his siblings. If not, he would never see any of them again. Being with Asadour helped. A thought flashed of little Walter and imaginary life in America. He fantasized about a place with no Turks to boss him around or taunt him. The thought buoyed him with—not courage, exactly—but something close. It was enough to believe he would find his way and speak those funny languages. Without the tiniest inkling of what might lie ahead, he fingered a piece of paper in his pocket on which was scrawled an address in a city called New York and pressed his face into the biting, westerly wind.

CHAPTER 4

OUT OF SYRIA
Mediterranean Sea - 1904

ASADOUR OF BEDROS

He finally slept. I was glad to see it. Frankly, I had begun to worry about my brother. Hovsep was wound up so tightly I feared he would snap in front of the authorities at Iskenderun port. In an irrational state of panic, he insisted on booking onto a transport that did not stop in Constantinople, which seemed rather hopeless as we came to learn that most steamers transitioning west through the Mediterranean routinely pass through that major port. But Hovsep was adamant. I have seen stubbornness in my younger brother before, but never with such determination about anything as his goal to avoid further interaction with the Turkish race. The bribes paid on our behalf when we embarked—we did not have the required passports to leave the empire—might not have covered us at another port. Thank God we prevailed, blessed to encounter a freighter steaming directly to Patras and once there, I noticed Hovsep audibly exhale.

Now, back at sea, he even smiled at the young crew boy, Suhail, who snuck us biscuits and tea from Captain's quarter this morning. Meals were not included with our fourth-class passage. It appears, too late, that we would have been better signed on as crew.

I know Hovsep is not oblivious to the pretty islands we are navigating among; the whitewashed houses clinging to tumbling cliffs—the clay rooftops blue, like some in Kessab, although these match closer to the deeper hue of the sea here than the water back home on the Syrian coast. I am aghast at how the sea water changes colors as we pass by Rhodes, Thera, and lastly, Athens, and am tempted to call out to my brother not to miss such mystery. But Hovsep still missed the sleep of two nights and a day and a half. I am hoping he will sleep all the way to Italy.

As for me, I cannot contain myself. I know it is sinful to be grateful for Hovsep's tribulation—good Lord, he has lost everything he knows and loves in less than a day. It is not Hovsep's nature to step off a cliff without some calculation and planning. Likewise, I know he would not have imagined his future elsewhere. Sure, he disliked the city and would have preferred to farm in the hills surrounding Kessab or back at the home gardens by the Kaladouran beach rather than endure the shoe shop with the elders. He envied me in escaping that world even while he saw no value in a life of books. But I doubt he ever would have imagined a life away from the family. And here we are, without a clue what we will find or where we will land. For myself... let's just say I have been granted a blessing.

Life in Ladehkiya for me could not have been sustained; the realization is dawning on me with every knot of sea that separates me from home. Perhaps I could not have allowed myself to consider it until this moment—this opportunity that has presented itself with sudden force. I am too different from anyone I have ever met: the Christian Syrian boys, the Muslims even less—perhaps, even among my own family. I would ultimately die back there, I know it now. But maybe, just maybe, in the bigger world we are entering, who knows what and who is to be discovered? My stomach quivers, heart flutters, eyelids dare not close for fear of missing the single scene that might transpose my wretched, yet hopeful, life. Ah, we will dock in Augusta, Suhail tells me, and have a day or two to wander around the Italian island—a place I have read much about. Blessed be the sun and stars shining upon us!

Sicily is so lovely to behold and even better to linger at. Hovsep joins me in long walks up the hills overlooking the sea. I know it reminds him of Kaladouran; after all, the same ocean laps its coiled surf onto the shorelines that contains it. But this is also quite different. You can see for miles across sprawling landscapes and rolling hills whereas at home, our Celderan Mountain blocks all sight beyond the beach. You would have to climb and reach the gardens to see the surrounding world. In this pastoral place the people we meet are so simple and joyous, easy to interact with in spite of language.

Hovsep buys a hand-woven scarf from a young girl we happen upon in the square surrounding a village fountain. She is likely a teen, but dressed so casually compared to Armenian girls with a low cut fluffy bodice and black eyes that truly sparkle. Her cheeks flush; she is clearly smitten with my handsome brother.

"*Prego*?" He does not know the proper word but has picked up this generic one.

"*Du`-e*." She charges him only a couple of lira, surely a mistake. But Hovsep rewards her with his dimpled grin, causing her to blush and giggle, and appear happy for the blunder.

Hovsep admires the orchards of fig, olive, and apple trees. Farmers shrug and even smile when we approach and indicate to them with our hands a desire to stroll the gardens and rows. He bends over greens and inspects luscious tomatoes drying on their vines and almost past picking. When we reach the gnarly fences covered with riotous grapevines, I ask him if he could see himself settling here to farm.

"Nah, it's not far enough… Damn Turks will come eventually." He looks over at me.

"I think Amirka, Asadour. We have a face there to welcome us!" and he pulls out a slip of paper from his baggy pocket, waves it triumphantly in the air before carefully tucking it back inside his trousers.

"So far away, Hovsep? Surely, Europe will be easier to adjust?"

"Think, Asadour! Everything little Walter told us of it…and there is true freedom a whole ocean away from the Ottoman world…"

It is the first time he's spoken of it. I have contemplated bringing up the incident, but I know better than to rush Hovsep. Not thirteen days from home and I am aware of how tense our lives had been under the Ottoman thumb. Roaming a mere few blocks from the Armenian quarter could spark random trouble at any moment of the day. I am fearful for my younger brothers Khatchig and Manas—especially Manas with his often explosive urges to react, worse even than Hovsep's natural impulses. We have left them to fend for themselves. But who knows? Perhaps we will discover a life that they can join and thrive in, along with us. Our sisters, however, I will not mention to Hovsep. Who knows their fate beyond marriageable age, never ours to guess? I wonder, too, at this moment, how might being *odar* feel in these new places? I suppose we will have some clues all too soon.

Suhail has warned us of potential problems in Marseille. First of all, it is good that we did not purchase passage directly from agents in Syria, or we might have been swindled. Second, it is customary that passengers from the Levant must quarantine for two weeks on the filthy island a kilometer from the port—Frioul—where we would certainly become ill if not already so. We are fortunate for the crew's custom of storing extra forms of exemption to be used in emergency for last-minute staff changes. We gladly tipped him for the carefully filled out papers that certified clean examinations performed prior to boarding. I can only imagine the setbacks that other passengers are faced with in France.

The sail across the western Mediterranean is surprisingly shorter than from the eastern end to Italy. In less than a full day we are skirting the coast of France, the lights of Nice twinkling in the black depths of night but the beaches that follow are shrouded in too much darkness to make out. By dawn, the port of Marseille is in sight. This time my brother and I stand side by side on deck, choosing silence for quite some time as we try to come to terms with the future or, rather, its vast unknowing space up ahead. I doubt we are sharing similar thoughts. But I am also proud to share my knowledge of geography with my younger brother, who is stuck in some bit of shock and not as excited as I to identify passing clusters of streetlamps as cities.

"You see there, Hovsep? In the night we saw Nice, and now we approach the big city—Marseille!"

Hovsep stares at the dock as it nears ever closer. Is he seeing impending doom, regretting the week that brought us to these planks on the opposite side of the Mediterranean Sea? With all my heart I hope not, and I touch his arm, causing him to look in my direction with a loving nod. That is assuring, at least. With a grind and three or four bumps, the boat jockeys to a halt and voices lobby back and forth while lines are thrown and caught. I allow my own elation, held in check for the last few moments in deference to what Hovsep may be feeling, to now march a slow rise to my upper chest.

In one way, I am also disappointed to reach a dense city world again. The idyllic peace we have enjoyed was a profound respite from stress, worry and, I suspect, the decisions and challenges to come. But now I must focus as we gather the few belongings we purchased in Catania. We both have jackets, thank God, and Hovsep has the pouch from home to carry a little food with us. I gratefully found another notebook in a market, crucial for my poems. It is leather bound and should weather whatever lies ahead. My brother had snickered at my purchase and I ignored him. It is true, we are afraid to part with the little cash we have, not sure how far we must get before finding some opportunity for earnings. But the people, the smells and sights, all that I witness; these things are jamming up my head and filling my conscious with content to a point that if I do not write out my impressions and thoughts I will explode in agony. I shake myself into the moment at hand. We must disembark on this busy dock. Hovsep asks Suhail for a clue where to find food and lodging.

Another crewman on ship overhears us and offers advice. "If you are looking for ships to the west, for New York Harbor, you must get to port at Le Havre in the north. You'll first need a train to Paris. Most who sail from this port are heading to points south…" Then as an afterthought, he calls to our backs as we continue, "And best to spend your money on the train rather than lodging – you can sleep on it!"

This seems like sound advice though I must say I would enjoy spending a night in Marseille first. Before I can catch my breath, I find myself trailing Hovsep, skipping steps to catch up, as he strides decisively up stone pathways that climb away from the seaport, seeking the train depot. Surprisingly, between the docks and the station we pass plenty of Arabic stalls and, my mouth beginning to taste the saliva of hunger, I implore my brother to pause long enough to buy some kibbee. The meat and bulgar patties will fill our stomachs for breakfast and hold us for a while. Hovsep gulps down two patties while still walking. I groan and run to keep up with him, pocketing one of mine for a calmer moment of digestion. At last, the station looms ahead. The trains are numerous and expensive. Hovsep shocks me: he wants to grab the first train available. How does he think we will fare in Paris, arriving in the night with barely any money?

"Hovsep, would it not be better to catch an overnight train, sleep well, and deal with a new challenge by day? "

Even as I repeat the crewman's advice to my brother, I have already decided to relinquish the decision making on this journey for selfish reasons. I want to observe, to experience every moment as stress free as possible. Therefore, I will not waste energy in argument or discussion, but defer to the decisions of my slightly younger brother, for whom it is more natural to act and accept the consequences of his actions. But twice now, he has listened to reason and again relents. It is just morning. We buy tickets and head back to the docks where we had passed a queue for day workers. Hovsep asked the man at the table if the pay would be delivered by the end of the day.

Offended by the question, the short Frenchman retorted, "If your work deserves it!"

"We can work until dusk and no longer," my brother surprises me with this statement while I silently thank the Lord for the small bits of French we have learned at school. Although most schools are taught in French, it is not the language of our missionary teachers, nor their focus. But we did have classes to learn basic French. The Mission schools were required to include French language in the curriculum, I discovered while tutoring.

Dock work is taxing and there is no place to store our jackets and outerwear, so we wrap these things around our waists. We haul boxes from grey or rusty containers to train carts, from gangplanks to lines, and from arms to arms along human queues spitting forth a variety of language. Sweating profusely by the time the sun disappears behind rooftops and the smokestacks of the larger ships in dock, we collect our francs and dash off to the station. Inside the station we buy bread and tea and settle into the train car with fifteen minutes to spare. We would not see the French countryside while we slept but we would awaken in "The City of Lights." I fall asleep pinching myself that I am soon to see Paris with my own grey Armenian eyes!

Before I open them again, my senses are assailed with that best of all smells that has greeted us since the day we were born and in every land or city we have since passed through on this journey—hot bread! The only detail that varies is the vendors' language of call. By now the French phrases sound more familiar, resembling the guttural Arabic from the back of the throat and, in that filmy haze just before full consciousness, I believed I was hearing the Muslim call to prayer that has punctuated our every morning wakening since the family move to Ladehkiya in my ninth year. But no, this is a pleasant call to our stomachs as the train ground its squealing brakes into the Paris Metro. There would be no shortage of food to grab. Every kind of bread stall imaginable, even the flat bread of the Arabs which is fluffier than our dryer Armenian version. I glance over at Hovsep who is also straightening from the hunched position of sleep in the cramped cabin, and it is clear from the brightening of his eyes that he is inhaling the same joy.

We quickly learn that we'll have to pick our way to a smaller, more regional station to book the train for Le Havre. I beg my brother to slow our mission, spend some time in the parks we pass and linger on the pedestrian bridges that arc over the river called Seine. In response, Hovsep pivots slowly in a circle and gazes about him. I can tell that the beauty of the city does not escape him, yet does not necessarily capture him either. Perhaps he is not meant to appreciate city life, I now think. But bless his heart, he humors me, appreciating my companionship and witness to his journey, which becomes more of a mission with each passing day. Sitting on a park bench near the river, we speak of Amirka.

"There is work of many kinds, everyone has said so. And land to spare."

"Whoa, don't get ahead of yourself, Brother." I laugh.

"Asadour, outside of Kessab and our inherited plots, where else might a man begin fresh and build something? There is much open land there; any person can buy a piece of it to farm." These dreams he never shares with me in any elaborate way, only mentions in passing. But I think I know his fantasies. He actually seems to envision farms that can feed whole villages!

Meanwhile, our ears are exploding with the many languages punctuating the air. I become intrigued with the clothing adorning the people bustling around us, offering so much to look at. The long skirts of women are of such a variety of swishy fabrics—I try to imagine Mary's reaction if she could witness these—and the bodices are fitted inward with tucks and pleats and gathers, creating quite a pleasant figure of the upper bodies. I'd never seen or imagined tiny umbrellas, but girls and women carried them rather gracefully and these, too, varied in fabric, color, size, and style. As for the feast of men's hats that abounds, we encounter only an occasional Ottoman fez, reason indeed to rejoice. We two sons of shoemakers cannot help but gaze downward at the boots, both of ladies and men, and for once I find myself grateful to be born of the trades. I feel no shame for our good quality leather shoes—shoes designed to last through multiple seasons. It seems as if people from every land have gathered in this magical place, and I would be very content to stay here to seek out the poets and painters that must be tucked away in the various alleys and courtyards that meander endlessly. I could not, however, abandon Hovsep on his mission. After all, I owe my blessed escape to his unfortunate circumstances.

And so, we walk and listen to the clops of horse hooves, the blare of horns, the clang of streetcars, the voices—oh, the voices! Vendors, women, children, men, cafes spilling people onto the sidewalks with cups and pastries at hand and chatter floating about their heads. We especially enjoy observing the seduction of the flower sellers.

"*Les fleurs, Monseur!*"

"*Oui, allors. Je veux les roses...*"

We sit just once for tea, and purchase bites from the carts and baskets of various vendors and girls while we explore streets and alleys. Best of all, as the sun drops low, lights such as I've never seen blink from every street corner, lit one by one at dusk by jolly men on bicycles.

"Now there's an enjoyable job," I laugh. I could have strolled all night long, but we eventually find ourselves at the smaller Gare and count out our few francs for the Le Havre local. A short ride later, we are in a ship queue at the massive port.

As we reach our turn in the line of fashionably dressed bodies, I hear Hovsep say a strange name to the ticket seller: "Josef Bedros!" Although stunned, I cannot ask him what he was doing in the moment because instead I am now in front of the man and must give my own name. In that vaguely, curious, unlimited space of time between inhaling, parting my lips, and releasing words from them, I realize that I have in my power the opportunity to reinvent myself! Hovsep had just done so, after all, so it seems the most natural fun of my life.

"Assad Tandee," I stammer out a combined Arabic and French identity, as imaginative as I can muster in the fleeting second, before I bravely glance at Hovsep's raised eyebrow and suppressed smirk. Names inscribed onto a large ledger, tickets in hand, we are fortunate in our timing and are allowed to embark at once. Our bunk is in steerage but gratefully, we have deck access and look forward to nine days of fresh sea air in our lungs.

CHAPTER 5

ENIED

Atlantic Ocean - 1904

ASADOUR OF BEDROS

The very next September morning, *La Gascogne* makes its way out of the harbor at dawn. "Josef" and I are at the rails already, studying the pewter-colored waters of the Atlantic Ocean. Hovsep—I mean Josef—leans back into the wind and howls, the roar is deep from his belly. It is the first time I have witnessed him laugh out loud since the passing of our mother Tzaghir four years ago. Heart pounding, I never knew such joy was possible.

The days run together. Hovsep so naturally strikes up conversations. He has discovered ways to get included in card games with off-duty crew members. Many of these are Arabs from northern Africa and language is no barrier. He even took on some chores to pay off debts as they occurred, but carefully pockets any winnings. I am delighted at the lightening of his soul. He is quickly transforming into a whole new person, free of burden and sorrow, and deepening in purpose with each day that passes. The ship is huge, and we are totally isolated from the upper classes of French and American families in the ornate dining rooms that I once peeked at through a grate on deck. We hardly care. We are so few days from our new life that these days at sea hardly matter. We are eighteen and seventeen and the world will lay at our feet when we dock in New York.

The sound of feet pounding from above is increasing as I shake my head into wakefulness. In seconds, understanding sweeps through me.

"Hovsep! It is now! Wake up!" We grab jackets and pouch and race to deck, pushing our way through bodies with abandon, as if we'd never been taught manners. Everyone has gathered on this deck to see the harbor come into view and finding a crack at the railing takes another five minutes of jostling and shoving, for which I do feel a twinge of shame. But that is forgotten as soon as I rest my elbows on the cold steel and take in several islands inching closer. When the stone lady is in sight, and Hovsep remains transfixed on her, I find myself gazing along the rail to either side of us and studying the faces floating above it. I can see the emotions in all these pairs of eyes, and I am overcome. How is it that so many can be buzzing with this same surge of energy in one single moment? My chest is going to burst with it. It. What is it? Hope? I'm not quite sure, but I will embrace it. Hovsep and I now share a good look at one another and a long, slow smile grows between us as we reach for one another and embrace. I feel the tears on his whiskers merge with my own.

There are several ships anchored and docked. The island in the harbor is so small that the passengers from all the ships seem to fill every inch of land from within and without the large terminal structure. Human lines continue from inside and spill out, winding along the shores where supervised arrivals linger and await instructions. I swear more than two thousand people weave a maze through the cavernous hall, separated by metal railings and as many voices bounce off ceilings that reach to the sky. I can see the sound aggravates Hovsep. This brother of mine—the new Josef Bedros—has been re-infected with the impatience that is consistent with his nature and our present predicament is tortuous for him. He paces, glares, and sighs loudly enough for anyone to hear.

"Hovsep, please sit—relax! Nothing you can do will make the time pass sooner!" I do not feel sorry for him, but annoyed. If only there were a card game allowed on the grassy area we are glued to. I sit down and fold my knees to my chest.

"I can't help it. This is… not civilized. What do they want from us? From everyone here? Why must it take so long with each person?"

I have no answer, of course. I could not know the process, only presume that we would have a quick physical examination and some questions about name and age. Someone in the line says that the examinations take only six seconds, if you are lucky. The sun is hot for the end of September, almost like a summer afternoon in Kaladouran, and we have been waiting since the dawn arrival. I look around for a face that might reveal a language I could communicate with. I silently wish my brother would be struck with the sort of lighthearted camaraderie he had enjoyed on the ship and look around again as if one of the ship's crew might magically appear to rescue us from this inconvenient dilemma. But all I see are faces more frightened than ours, more confused, and so much more susceptible to the unknown than even I am feeling. Still, none seem as damned frustrated as my wound-up brother.

It was a day and a half before our turn came. We slept on the floor of the great terminal and gulped down the meager food offerings brought around twice that day by workers in green uniforms. They carried crates of wrappings in which we found thin meat slices wrapped in bread, which I learned are called sandwiches. They passed these out and followed with urns of tea and coffee to wash away our thirst. We devoured our sandwiches in two bites but for these we were grateful. Hovsep laughed at the thought that the ship food had been a luxury we will miss. The line in front of us dwindles to about fifty people by mid-morning, and finally we are thrust to the edge of a cold, brown table while a family of six persons ahead of us are led away to a room from the side of the table that offered no view from our position. A man with hair only at the two sides of his ears, and no mustache, is seated behind the table. He grunts a question I cannot not make out. When we do not respond, he looks up impatiently, tapping the end of a pencil on the flat surface in front of the table.

"No English?" he demands and when we shake our heads, he sighs like a person who has seen too much in this world and must still endure. "What, then?"

"Turkish? Armenian? French?" I list all these choices in French, hoping something would help.

The man shrugs and calls out to someone unseen from the other direction. Then he points to me with his pencil, jabbing it toward my chest to indicate my identity. Name? I must struggle to remember the name I have invented just ten days prior at the other side of the ocean.

"Assad Tandee." I try, but fail, to stifle a cough.

He looks up sharply, then lowers his eyes and shuffles through loose pages, until he makes a mark of chalk on one of them—an "E". Another man appears suddenly and motions for me to follow. I follow him tentatively into the mysterious room that the family had previously entered, glancing back at Hovsep who is rooted very still and watching me with an unusual quality of concern. I shrug my shoulders at him and continue through the doorway, hoping we will be reunited within moments. There is just enough time to hear my handsome brother turn back to the bald man and repeat his new name.

"Josef Bedros." The name he uses is an English translation of Hovsep that the missionaries once mentioned in a class on the English language. He had naturally added his middle name. All of my brothers and I share the same middle name, the name of our father. I now wish I had chosen such a simple new identity.

Once inside, the man indicates a bench to sit on, and picks up a tray of instruments before turning to me. He listens to my heart with a cone shaped tube I have seen many times before, when the doctor came from the Armenian quarter to attend to one or another of my brothers and me. And when Mayrig gave birth to baby Marta... I catch my breath and still my mind as he shines a light in my eyes, followed by my ears, and back to my eyes again. He asks a question I cannot understand and so I shake my head. He reaches with both hands to physically turn my head towards a wall where there is tacked a paper with some markings. He asks another question, then walks to the paper and taps on a marking. He seems to want me to read it. But I cannot see it, not in any language. I make a guess though, reciting a letter in French as confidently as I can, praying he is not a French speaker and might assume my response to be correct. Instead, his brow scrunches a bit, and he points to another mark above the first one. Again, I make a wild guess, this time more loudly, faking a confidence I do not have. The man frowns and returns to my side. With an instrument like a hooked needle, he lifts my eyelids one at a time and once more shines his light ray into each of my eyes. I reflexively cough again, and the man appears to jump back a bit.

He leads me out of the room, back to the table, and exchanges words with the bald man. Now a sliver of nervous twinge begins in my groin, and I pray for Hovsep to emerge from the room where surely he was being examined. The bald man stands up and walks down the room along the wall nearest to us where he taps on the shoulder of one of a cluster of men standing by another door. The man is very tall with a clipboard at his side and turning, practically has to bend over to hear the shorter man whisper into his ear. The two men turn back toward us, just as Hovsep appears from the room, and the man who had examined me slips by him. Hovsep shoots me a look of relief, as if all had

51

gone well, but my nervousness is beginning to spread from my groin to my stomach. The two men arrive back at the desk where the bald man sits down just as he calls out to the next persons in line.

The tall man looks at me and puts his hand on my back to guide me away from the desk. I look over my shoulder in time to see Hovsep stiffen and follow us. The door which the man had come from, farther down the room, opens up and he gently pushes me through it, though not unkindly, so that I am not alarmed though still nervous. Hovsep shoves his way into the room and stays close beside me from that moment on.

This man has blue eyes, silvery short hair and, I now notice, a sort of military or government uniform which I could not identify. He pulls up a chair, indicates for me to sit and begins to speak.

"Arabic?" he asks it in English, and I am not sure of the meaning. Then he repeats it in French and I nod with relief.

"You will not be admitted to the United States." I can hear nothing further. I do not even comprehend that the man has switched to some dialect of Arabic that is barely recognizable to Hovsep and me. The sickness in my stomach has crawled to my chest, and I think I might faint. I do not dare look at my brother beside me, and wish from the bottom of my soul that he did not need to hear the words that followed.

"You have a condition in your eye that is not acceptable. I am sorry. You will be held in this place until we can find a spot for your passage back."

Now my brother is spluttering, urgently, "No, not back! Any place else... please?" The man looks down at him, pauses.

"You are together? Family?"

Hovsep nods. The man who has changed our lives in less than a minute looks at us silently for a moment. He is not a cruel man. Somehow, I know this. I actually find myself wondering how or where he has learned his halting Arabic.

"There are some options I can suggest."

CHAPTER 6

TROPICS

Caribbean Sea - 1904

JOSEF

The man looming over them might as well have kicked his gut and placed a granite boulder on his chest, holding him down, constricting…. He couldn't find a breath. Hovsep heard a moan escape his own mouth, then closed it instantly having glanced at Asadour's crushed face. Are we helpless? He could not accept that. He looked hard into the man's face which actually showed a bit of pity for them, written all over wide cheeks and cloudy eyes. Through a drowning sensation like sinking underwater, Hovsep managed to hear voices, at first distorted, and slowly became aware that the man was offering something, something to grab hold of. He grasped at a prick of hope, as if struggling upwards toward light, and heard his own squeezed voice whimper, "What sort of options?"

"Some fellas in your position find their way to the islands." It was hard to make out the man's Farsi Arabic. "I don't know about work, but the restrictions are negligible and if you don't want to return to your country..."

"We cannot return! Please, how do we do this?" He had come fully awake now.

Passage on a low-cost freighter leaving two days later was arranged, with the man's assistance: destination, Santo Domingo. The brothers were not permitted to leave the detention compound until departure and slept on the ground for two nights. It was cold but tolerable, not quite October, and dry enough that they did not chill. The jackets served as pillows, and Hovsep could still smell the girl in Sicily who had sold him his scarf when he offered it to Asadour, who refused. On the second morning, no sooner than their eyes opened, the man returned. Hovsep could not decide whether to hate him for his message or thank him for his help as he walked them personally to the dock and communicated with some uniformed staff. They were taken on as crew, deck cleaning for him, mess hall prep for Asadour, which suited each of them just fine. Hovsep preferred the fresh air on deck and the hours away from conversation—for now—with his brother. At least they had bunks, hard as they were, and hammocks on deck to sleep in when the boat reached the southern seas and nights grew too stifling to sleep below decks.

Hovsep did not know what he should say to his brother, or if he wanted to say anything as yet. Instead of making their way through the streets of New York, the two were on a freighter headed south. Asadour was most likely drowning in guilt, having closed that door on them. He was at a loss of how to cheer or assure him—or if he wanted to. He had no desire to speak, not until he could identify what he was feeling, and then temper it so that his insides didn't rain down on Asadour. The disappointment was not yet processed, lying in wait, fresh and paralyzing. Stunned into stillness, Hovsep gazed at the passing shorelines visible in the distance at certain points when the ship ventured west of the darker colored current beneath the water. Omer, the crewman from Syria, told him it was called Gulf Stream, and the ship was small enough that they could steer west of it sometimes, and hug the coast while approaching the first port of call. The land behind the shoreline appeared eerily flat and mountainless. Only at one stretch of shoreline in France had he seen, from the sea, beaches without tree lines with their purple shadows splashing from the lowering sun, nor windy hills with blue roofs and whitewashed huts rising beyond the sand.

So this is Amirka. Where are the mountains? Where were they going? What will they do in the islands? Most of the crew spoke French or Spanish. Omer, of course, spoke to the brothers in his native Arabic. He surprised them with the information that there were quite a few Arabs in Dominican Republic. Hovsep tried to make out whether this was a good thing or bad thing. His mind still dazed in disappointment, he shook his head to focus. What could be done? He could not abandon his brother who had left home for no other reason than to accompany him toward his fate. Now their fates had taken a turn together. With any luck, he might block thoughts for some time—just as he had when crossing that other sea, the Mediterranean.

The wind became balmy, soothing. Hovsep spent all the day and night on deck, except for meals, talking as much as possible with the crew and practicing words of Spanish they shared with him. Asadour was actually smiling a lot and appeared happy to be going to a warm place. Salt air seemed to nudge energy into his being, but Hovsep felt lulled and lazy by it; something like a dull impatience was building. He told himself to resist the mental distraction and 'get on with it,' shaking his head and stamping a foot, while his insides screamed that he was moving in the wrong direction, away from his destiny.

Hovsep and Asadour were not allowed off ship at the only port it anchored, since they were still in the United States—somewhere called *Borfort...Sa-oot Karolaina*? Shoving off once more, there was only ocean for a day and a half, no more land to see in the distance. They would disembark when the Spanish port was reached. Finally, the water evolved into lighter, varying colors of blue as the boat navigated shallow depths between small islands. And then a large land mass surrounded by the prettiest green blue... The boat screeched to a slow crawl and the brothers glued their eyes over the rails to what looked like sand only meters below. It was deceptive, they discovered. The crew yelled excitedly, Omer among them. Asadour called out to him, asking if this was Santo Domingo.

"No. But north of Hispaniola the water is very deep."

When the boat later came upon another shoreline, this time of a much larger landmass, the brothers asked him again.

"We are on the northern banks now. Not Santo Domingo, no. But we will sail farther east and around the island to the southern side to dock. Too bad, Samana can be fun." Omer chuckled, suggesting something unspoken.

The air was suddenly punctuated with shouts: "*La baleine!*" "*Ballena!*" from crew on the starboard side; the brothers rushed to the join the cluster of men pointing over the side of the boat. The huge, sleek creature—no three, four—breaching, then skimming alongside the freighter, water spouting in intermittent bursts. Omer explained the pod of whales that mate in Samana Bay every winter.

"It is early now, but soon they will fill the bay," he said.

Slowly rounding the eastern point of the island, every beach, every building along the coastline was visible. Hovsep surprised himself with the pang of excitement at the sight of the peaceful hamlets they smoothly glided by. How pleasant it must be to relax on a porch such as those half-hidden behind swaying palms while still receiving enough of breezes feathered through the fronds. Finally, a large dock with five or so vessels came into view, amidst crowded, mostly single-story, wooden buildings. Hovsep immediately noticed the structures topped with tile roofs of red clay, contrasting the blues of the Mediterranean.

The boat was tied off and secured, and they were given instructions. With nothing to collect but the jackets around their waists, much too hot to wear, they finished the job unloading containers and immediately moved on down the dock, not looking back. The brothers walked, not verbalizing that most obvious question: what next—to do or eat, where to work or sleep. A city! At least navigating this one might be simpler than the cities left behind.

Omer shouted from behind Asadour, running breathlessly toward them. "Youssif! Wait! Be careful how you talk to the people!" He caught up and bent over, trying to catch a breath.

"What do you mean?" Asadour beat Hovsep to the question.

"Save your Arabic for the Syrians you meet. The natives call us 'smelly Turks,' and will not help you if you approach them with guttural words. How much Español can you speak?"

Hovsep groaned and smacked his palm to his head. "God damn it! We've run away from Turks only to be mistaken for them?" This was a cruel joke.

"Listen, just come with me. We are laying over until morning. I'll help you find food and a place to sleep tonight."

The brothers gratefully followed Omer north from the dock at the Rio Ozama past the Parque Duarte and Parque Colon as he pointed out these places and names and led them to a bodega pub he was familiar with. He also explained about the Turkish thing.

"All the Syrians here are Christian, like me, and have also fled the Turkish nonsense. But the first of us arrived about twenty years ago with official documents from the Ottoman Empire, so the locals referred to them as Turks... And smelly because, well, many of them live in dismal circumstances, sometimes fifteen to thirty in a house."

Hovsep cringed, but Asadour seemed as fascinated as he was with everything new, and curiously immune to the impact of being *odar* in a strange new land. It seemed most of the Arab boys—all young men or even teenagers—were vendors, taking their wares to the streets and countryside, evidently the fastest and easiest way to make income. Hovsep's mind began to process the steps to set up an enterprise, calculating the need to study merchandise and costs. Then, of course, how to avoid Arabs or be mistaken for one. The first step would be their names. The crew had already helped with this, he suddenly realized.

"Asadour, you will be *Stefano*. I am *José*."

One month later, Hovsep stood on this new beach, already as familiar to him as this new ocean, and kicked at a clump of sand. Asadour was sixty meters away, bargaining with a customer. Hovsep hardly glanced at them. Stubborn, stubborn, pig-headed brother! Hovsep was convinced that his plan to move into the rural hills with an expanded product pool—sewing trinkets and necessary cooking items—would triple their income.

But Asadour wanted to stick to the Playa Montesinos where competition with new arrivals, typically Syrians hailing from Bayruth to Tripoli, was quickly increasing. And the locals were so unwelcoming it was only a matter of time before they might be run off the public beach with other vendors. Selling items from a blanket on the beach by the docks of one city was not going to sustain them. Why was Asadour digging in? And why did he seem so listless and uninterested to explore the island's countryside? Nor was his brother sleeping well and often awoke coughing, which stung Hovsep with worry that he didn't know what to do with. So he trained his attention on planning.

Hovsep...Josef, Youssif—he could hardly keep up with his evolving names—was called José by the local boys in the beach community. He liked the simplicity of the name and mused about it while strolling further down the water line and noting that, in spite of the tide receding, the waves continued their steady roar. He was actually pacing more than strolling, sensing his impatience to get on with life. At times this beach soothed him; other times it just reminded him that he was stuck in one spot. Yet, he stopped to listen for a moment.

"*El Mar Atlantico*." He practiced saying it in his mind, wishing he had the English version already for the greater container of this Caribbean Sea. Learning

Spanish presented yet another roadblock in front of the inevitable stab at English in his future. None of his homeland languages (Kessabtsi, Turkish, Arabic) helped toward either of these, except perhaps a bit of French. He actually enjoyed the Spanish tongue.

Meanwhile, he had to get off this God forsaken beach hawking wares to new immigrants and city residents who neither needed nor wanted them. Mostly, José longed to stretch his spirit and legs in the hills and meet up with country folks who knew how to grow a vegetable and spoke carefully but with clear meaning. They would have use for needles, pans, and boot soles. He had located a cart to refurbish and needed only a donkey. It would be the fastest solution to the new plan. He allowed himself a pang of regret that he could not board a steamship on the opposite dock and head back to New York. But he could not. Any idea of abandoning Asadour filled him with shame.

The thoughts screaming in his head slowed as the wind whipped up the surf. He looked out once more at the big gray Atlantic and made a decision. He would take to the interior hillside with or without Asadour. If his brother refused they could split the profits and part work routes. He could come and go as needed for supplies, and they would spend time together on those days.

CHAPTER 7

ᗪOMINICANO

Hispaniola - 1907

JOSÉ

"José! *Gracias y vienes de nuevo! No se demora*!" Tomas called back as José led the packed mule toward the path beyond a leaning wooden gate that had never known the protection or color of a coat of paint.

"*Si, claro! Hasta luego*!" José waved over his head without looking back.

He liked this family with whom he had spent a good five days to participate in their "*junta*," enjoying meals and laughter with extended village folk who had gathered to help erect a new stable and mill at the lush, green fields that hugged a bend of the Yuma River. All of the participants had purchased at least one solid item from his cart. José had established a custom to deliver a free needle for each purchase, a practice that endeared him to what became repeat customers and also opened doors to him in new villages as word spread across the echoing valleys. Tomas' family and neighbors had joked and worked together with light-hearted eagerness and the hours had flown by. Evenings were even better: platters of rice, beans, greens, and roasted pig (José preferred the taste of lamb but this was not a common option on the island); lastly, a smoldering fire and handmade local cigars for which Tomas' wife was famous. Before bed, José joined the inevitable game of dominoes; the wooden pieces had dots carved out and filled with fading paint to represent various numbers.

"You can't be much of a Turk, playing the game so well without cheating," joked Tomas.

"If you ever call me a Turk again, I'll beat you out of all your money, then steal your horse!" This sort of banter was common among Dominicans but rare among strangers, José a clear exception.

The freedom in the central valley and mountains was exhilarating. He knew that large bands of Syrians occupied the territories nearest the border with Haiti, and he never went that far west in the highest peaks, establishing his own reputation as an alternative to the Arab vendors—or Turks, as the Dominicans referred to them. Occasionally he met up with a Syrian or two traveling solo or in pairs and joined them over a fire for a meal and perhaps a card game. The first season he had left Asadour on the beach in Santo Domingo and headed east past sugar cane fields to San Pedro de Macoris to load supplies. This was where most of the Syrians were based and useful information was available, along with the provisions.

José had been schooled with Christian Syrians and could find common ground with the Syrian immigrants of the island. He slid easily into conversation with individuals. But he avoided bands, especially the large groups of Arabs that clustered in the Sierra de Neiba. He preferred to travel solo, ever gaining more of the local language and letting it be known he was NOT a 'smelly Turk' peddler. He'd been at it for two years and repeatedly found warm welcome, and most always a bed, among the Dominicans he befriended.

Before the approaching Christmas season, José awoke one morning weary of walking, and weary of his donkey that was so ambivalent it didn't even bray back at him when he talked to it out of loneliness. Mind floating away from him, he thought about the preparations that Mary would be making in the big kitchen at home and the feasts to come at Kaladouran and Kessab, and immediately berated himself for allowing such memories to surface. He realized that he was missing his brother acutely and decided to pack up earlier than he had planned for Santo Domingo. But the surprise return visit alarmed him.

It had been months since he last entered the city, and Asadour was not to be found. José had to ask around the neighborhood by the Plaza de Espana where they had last resided before he managed to locate his brother. Asadour appeared ill and was recovering in the house of a short Dominican woman who brought him rice and broth and pressed wet cloths to his face.

"Hovsep, the town passed an ordinance against 'Turkish' street sellers, and I could not convince them who I was. I had to give it up. I went to the sugar plantation and tried my hand at cutting sugar. But I couldn't keep up…"

The work in the fields was too grueling for him, which was concerning. If Asadour could not work the plantation, nor sell trinkets, what was left for him to subsist on? Meanwhile, it seemed Asadour was trying to teach a group of four young boys some phrases and words in French, as well as mathematical formulas.

"I use a combination of markings, hand gestures and French words, which usually falls on deaf ears," Asadour chuckled. "And this woman—her name is Leticia—and two of her neighbors, the mothers of the other three boys, they do much cooking and bring me meals."

He seemed quite content and assured his brother that he was on the mend and would be back on his feet in no time. But José was anxious to have a conversation with his brother; he felt it timely. Stopping in San Pedro de Macoris, he had joined a card game with some Syrians and learned some news that excited him. Two things, really.

"Asadour, I have a plan. Hear me out! Do you know you can take a ship to South Amirka? I think we hit the jackpot! Forget about this island. We can get you passage on the Booth Line, out of Lisbon. It comes to the West Indies and then on to Brazil. That will get us out of these islands to the real world. We may have to work some more, but we can save enough."

"You also, Hovsep?"

"My plan is still New York. You see, a fellow told me that Puerto Rico—the island after this one—is part of the United States. I don't want to take a chance going through that intake building again; maybe our records are there and they will stop me. But if I crew or travel by ship from Puerto Rico, it could dock without customs. I can maybe slip off the boat without papers…. that is what the guy said!"

"But Hovsep, Brazil? Where will I go? What will I do there?"

"There are Kessabtsis in Sao Paolo. Maybe even cousins by now. Let's write home and find out the news and see what guys may have gone to America already. We'll send it with the mail boat tomorrow."

José decided in that moment that he wanted to spend more of his time with Asadour, but he also needed to save enough money for them both. It appeared that Leticia was quite devoted to his brother's health and José was grateful, knowing he could head back into the hills with his cart for the remaining dry months and leave him in good hands. But Asadour surprised him with an idea. When he brought it up, José thought his brother was going to faint, he was so flushed with excitement.

"I have my own idea, Hovsep. I want to return to Samana. Actually to Miches, near Samana. Leticia has family in that village and a cabin she can use and has agreed to take me there. Until we hear from Ladehkiya and purchase passage, I can teach the village children French and write my poetry."

José paced for about two minutes, thinking, assessing, and arriving at no argument to dissuade Asadour. He could neither think of a negative consequence nor any better option to offer. "Fine, Asadour. But I will make the trip with you and continue inland from there."

It took only days to discover how much simpler, calmer life was in the northern coastal village. Growing grateful for his brother's decision, José watched Leticia hover around Asadour, whom she called 'Stefano', easing his own concern. And Asadour seemed to be recovering well. The night before he was to return to the central valley, the two brothers took a stroll and passed by a shop with a dark blue sign that read '*Zapatos*'. They winked at each other, turned back, and entered the familiar shoe shop with a sense of confident anticipation. The group of men inside was not entirely made up of Dominicans. A Frenchman, a Creole, and a Syrian were also present; the odd group of men seated around a table with little piles of the spotted ivory tiles the locals called dominos.

Looking up, the patron called, "*Se interesses? Vienes, sienta!*"

The game gave the men a chance to chat casually, warming to one another, especially when José expressed in their language that he and his brother were from a family of shoemakers. They became instant guests of honor, which included a tradition of the guest having the choice of game. José didn't hesitate. "Any cards in this house?"

Laughing, the shoemaker reached for a deck and threw it to him. "*Toma*, José!"

As the night progressed the Frenchman introduced himself as a doctor, also a poet; before leaving, he expressed some concern for Asadour's pallor and suggested he come round the next day so he could take a look. Since Asadour agreed, José alarmingly realized that his brother was still carrying some lingering illness, though he had hidden it well.

Later, as they returned to Leticia's bungalow and settled into two hammocks strung together in front of a window shrouded by palm leaves, José reflected that they might actually be in one of the huts he had admired from the freighter from New York two years earlier.

The woman and her son were asleep together on a single bunk in the only separated room, and Asadour tried to restrain his excitement in a whisper, "Hovsep, do you realize! Daniel has published two whole volumes of poetry and a third on the way! He is a true French poet."

"I thought he was a doctor." José saw an opening into the discussion he wanted to have.

"Yes, but not exclusively. Why did God bless and guide us to this community? I am overjoyed with inspiration. I will finally write my poems."

"But Asadour, who will read poems in Armenian? Especially here…"

"Not Armenian. That is, not exclusively. Arabic is the universal language for poetry, Hovsep. I will be one of the great Arabic poets. And perhaps some French translations later on… so that I can share with the larger world."

José wished he did not have to leave and sighed, loving that his brother was animated once more and imagining how nice it might be to stay near him. But he was responsible for both of their passages to the future. He would leave the following day after a morning meal.

The brothers had already established a favorite hangout in Samana. The bakery also attracted some of their new friends and the next morning they walked there to join the men they had befriended. José led the donkey hitched to the two-wheeled cart that was laden with his packs and enough supplies for three months. He would enjoy breakfast and leave for the hills from there. The baker was Syrian. Over the cordial morning conversation, it was revealed to him that the brothers knew how to make pita bread in several versions: Armenian, Syrian, and Turkish. The man wished to expand his bread offerings and just like that, José found himself in a new line of work! His evening wish had been magically granted! Asadour would also work, although only half shifts. José was all too happy that he could watch over his unhealthy brother.

"This beats the long walking, though I will miss my friends in the country."

"Can you still go there once a week, or once a month? To balance things for you?"

"Nah, it's not worth keeping the mule fed. I'll sell the cart, too."

José found a buyer the following day, and a bonus, too: a neighbor of Leticia offered him a room to rent, including meals. The holidays were joyous, and the dry season felt easy and peaceful. Though José had enjoyed the peddler's life with a reckless freedom, he marveled at how lazy he felt these days, even working at a hot oven all day long. That year, Carnival arrived around José's February birthday and, with new friends and feeling part of the community, the brothers enjoyed themselves, exhilarated for perhaps the first time in their Caribbean lives.

Music and the smell of fried food filled the center of the town square. Most of the villagers wore at least partial costumes: some women in traditional gowns that were long with full skirts over petticoats in the colonial style, and the younger girls in varied styles, most holding masks on a long stick in front of their faces. The older men wore 18th century cravats and hosiery. Young men were dressed in more non-descript variations.

José laughed, whispering, "Where is a blasted fez when we could wear one and mock it?" The boys were standing on the outskirts of a cluster of villagers gathered in the square. José stood transfixed for a few moments while he admired a group of women dancing, black hair flying as they whirled past. A few of the girls smiled shamelessly at him when they caught him staring, and José grinned back. Just then a familiar face came bounding towards them.

"Omer! *Que pasa?*" José was genuinely delighted, giddy with happiness to see their old friend from the freighter.

The three young men moved away from the music and poured cups of rum from the bottle they ordered at a nearby bodega, chatting louder with every round of shots. José listened with full attention, while his cigarette burned down to meet his fingers. Finally, he released the question he had been suppressing, waiting for the right moment.

"Omer, do you know men who sail to New York by going through Puerto Rico? You know, without customs and checking papers?"

"Sure! Our freighter stops in San Juan on the way back from the British islands after we turn around from the southern continent. And you can take a mail boat from right here in Samana. But there are more boats from Santo Domingo, of course, going to San Juan. I would suggest that way."

José looked cautiously at Asadour. For some reason, he sensed the news was not so welcome to his brother's ears. "Do you think the time is coming?"

Asadour was silent for a moment. Did José imagine a gulp in his throat before he swallowed and faintly answered, "Yes, of course, God willing."

A silence expanded between them, its gulf signifying the inevitable.

The rainy season came, and José was more grateful than ever for the bakery. Trekking through the hills and mud with a stubborn mule was no longer something he wanted to endure, now that he had tasted a dry warm kitchen that provided a living. By now he was baking desserts—baklava, boorma, smeed (Syrian farina cake); these were all a big hit with the locals, not to mention the Syrians who came through. On certain days, as he pummeled dough into balls and rolled filo as thin as possible into flaky layers that would sandwich chopped nuts and syrup, José allowed himself to crawl into a secret world in his mind where he was 'Hovsep of the old country,' helping his mother bake. It was before his sisters were born and he was a natural at it; Mayrig always said so. When Mary was four, he began to show her what he knew of baking. By the time she was eight, he relinquished all baking to her and thought little more of it. He thought to himself now that, had he stayed in Syria, this line of work might have been an alternative to the shoe shop.

Never mind, damn it. He didn't stay in Syria and wouldn't stay on the Dominican island either. He decided that he needed to get to Santo Domingo to secure passage for Asadour on the Booth Line before he could plan for himself. His brother seemed not too concerned about leaving this island or starting fresh in the southern Latin countries. He truly enjoyed his friends, the children he taught, the care of a woman.... Yet it was his duty to deliver Asadour to the new world on one continent or another. He could not leave him here with no future.

As expected, Asadour was not enthusiastic when he brought it up that night. Yet he agreed to go to the Samana harbor the next day with José and inquire about the timetables for the shipping lines. They learned the next passage would be in mid-December. Santo Domingo to Caracao, Caracao to Belem, Rio de Janeiro and Sao Paolo. Leaving the harbor, the two sat for a rum at a seaside bodega shack.

"December it is. I will wait until you are safely boarded and then head to San Juan."

"No, no, no! Brother, there is no need for you to lose time and this chance. If you wait until the dry season, all the jobs in San Juan will be filled up. Or if you didn't stay there, the sail and landing north in the wintertime will be so cold, you will suffer terribly. You must make your move now. You will write me as soon as you arrive, before I sail, so that I'll have a way to send word from Sao Paolo."

Sensing a lingering reluctance on his brother's part, José swallowed and tentatively said aloud the question in his mind. "Are you in love, brother? Is that what's troubling you?"

Asadour took his time. No less curious, José remained patient, feeling rather tender toward his older brother. Finally, "Hovsep. It's... different. I mean... I love Leticia with all my heart. But not the way you imagine." He clearly struggled for the next words. "I do not think I am even capable. Not in the traditional way, I mean. I don't know..." His voice trailed off and landed in silence.

José wondered what Asadour meant by the vague words but thought better than to push him. It was more natural and comfortable to defer to Asadour's privacy. This brother had always seemed different in subtle ways, such as his love of book learning over physical games and play, or his tendency to withhold judgment from the most egregious of situations that infuriated the other brothers. Thinking now about it, Asadour's cheerful disposition underlined a kind of self-acceptance, even confidence. Perhaps this was due to the world of privacy he cloaked himself in. If only there was time to explore this overlooked layer— one which he had not appreciated before—of his brother, his best friend.

Parting with Asadour—there was no escaping it. He could not see himself accompanying Asadour to South America; he knew in his bones it was not his destiny. He had managed to tamp down the direct thought, distracting himself with goals and logistics, but there was no avoiding it now. The dull ache in his chest now seared through his stomach and into his groin. My God, could he really do it? Move on to worlds unknown, never to laugh and eat together again, sleep in a room together—he thought he might be sick. Asadour had slept near him since his earliest memories, the only exception being his months peddling the hills. Different though they were, they had been mostly inseparable. José had not said goodbye to all of his siblings in Ladekiyah nor to any cousins in Kessab. Now he would be severed from the last of his family and on his own. He would adjust, of course, just as he had surrendered life at home overnight. He wished he felt certain about leaving Asadour on this island. It was the only bit that nagged at him, and he wished he could swat away the lingering trace of unease.

CHAPTER 8

AMIRKA

Atlantic Ocean - 1908

JOSÉ

He caught a ride with a kind Dominican on a cart stacked with melons out of Sabana de la Mar. He had to shift his butt between the round balls of fruit, scooping melons onto his lap to remain secure enough not to constantly roll off and bruise himself. The rainy season, as promised, ensured a shower twice in the day and soaked José both times, between which he dried thoroughly under the blazing summer sun. A most uncomfortable ride, but he was on the way to his future, not just to work, and was plenty willing to suffer a little. The mule and cart had fetched a savings and, supplemented by six months of work in the bakery, was enough for two boat fares. José felt sure he had enough to make it this time. It was August and the heat scorched. José looked ahead and squinted into blinding haze, praying for a light breeze to kick up in that moment. He silently counted his money in his pocket and checked for the piece of paper. There was no turning back now, but the incessant unease of leaving Asadour on the Dominican island would never leave him.

The ferry to San Juan and immediate passage on the *S.S. Carolina* was the easiest portion of the journey since he had turned his back to Syria four years earlier. The steamer was 380 feet long and mostly full of sugar on this run to New York; there were only twenty-seven passengers. A unique group of people, José befriended each and every one of his fellow travelers over the six days at sea. He trotted out his true last name and logged passage as José Karamardian, twenty-two (exaggerated), Armenian. It felt exhilarating and adventurous to be partially his old self (Karamardian), partially his current self (José), and wondering what might become his permanent identity.

The Bancalari family from Italy were very gracious to him, even after he flirted with Rosa Ichenone, the young girl traveling with them as a nanny. Bartolo and Ana had two teenagers, a toddler, and an infant in Rosa's charge. He also tried to provide some company to the single Syrian woman named Maria Assise, twenty-six, who had been living in Puerto Rico since 1901. She was traveling to New York as an engaged woman and expressed some concern about appearances when conversing with José. But he sensed that speaking her native Arabic tongue was a temptation she could not resist, having been away from home for seven years.

"Youssif, you are educated, fluent in my language, Christian, and..." she actually told him, "astonishingly handsome when your smile splits into dimples."

He guessed that she considered the boat passage to possibly be her last moments of free interaction with males outside the family, and so succumbed to the charm of open conversation with him. It was nice to talk with her and learn more about what *odar* felt like to a woman in the islands. It was easy to be a perfect gentleman and yet converse so deeply, both parties aware of the unique opportunity suspended in space and time. They were sometimes seated near a Dominican couple headed to Paris and traveling with another couple, Gloria and Enrique Jimenez of Puerto Rico.

The remaining passengers were men traveling solo, all of whom rapidly developed into José's card team. Francesco Grullon from Santo Domingo, Celso and Lorenzo from Spain, the older Girolino Chieffo from Italy, and two Brits—Herbert Cloy, forty, and Allen Lane, twenty-seven, who were going to live in Halifax, Nova Scotia. When the sea was smooth, they set up their game on a deck table. More often they hunkered below, due to choppy conditions, where sometimes a cigarette, card, or drink glass slid around, or even off, the table. José would look around at the men, smoke forming a mushroom around their heads, and try to tune his ears to three simultaneous languages swirling about, weaving in and out of the floating smoke. The recognizable words at a card table are usually swear words in any language.

"*Basta!*"

"*Pega tutti, mi dio!*"

"My God! How can that be? I had the secret hand!" The Brits' understated exclamations were beyond José's grasp thus far. But the card game was universal, and he was the most relaxed he could remember since childhood in Kessab, when thoughts of future had yet to crowd out pleasures of the moment.

Meals with the group triggered his memory of family Sundays in Kaladouran, before the move to the city, when José, as Hovsep, had sensed the rightfulness of his seat at the table. Now perfect strangers ate together in the middle of a churning ocean. The chatter was bright, punctuated, and cheerful, as if a colorful wrapping enveloped a deep bond the group was feeling for the few days they were cast together, before parting to distant futures in various parts of the world. José reflected with warmth on Tomas' family on the Yumas River and recent friendships in Samana, but this briefer experience was more finely tuned, connected somehow to the sensation that there was something larger than the group and the boat that they were not entirely in control of. He would not welcome the feeling every time it appeared in life, but for this moment, in the days from August 25th to 31st in the year 1908, it was wholly embraced by his young, and as yet undaunted, spirit.

One month shy of four years since the last time José entered New York Harbor, the *S.S. Carolina* from San Juan glided right past the island of that nightmare. With every ounce of his being, he wished his brother were at his side now. Still, his shoulders relaxed so much he felt lightheaded, almost dizzy as the *Carolina*, with several attempts, squeezed itself into a space at the pier between two larger vessels. As the crew slipped the bowline around the pier cleat, José momentarily imagined hopping over the side onto the concrete like a crew member. Instead, he joined the group of young men clustering by the gangway and, not knowing what was happening, found himself moving with the bodies that had sandwiched him in the middle as the mass shuffled down the iron planks and right off the boat. He heard the first mate, Manuel, call to his back, "*Buena suerte,* José!" but he didn't look back.

Stretching his hand over his head in a wave gesture, José continued straight ahead and strove to maintain a steady stroll, terrified of being stopped at any second but willing himself to not believe it. About a dozen paces off the pier, he safely broke away and veered toward the trolley cars, horse carriages, and vehicles filling the streets. There he halted, did a slow turn, eyes raking in greys and browns of mountainous buildings. Where to begin? He looked around for clues, saw tall buses screeching through the intersection ahead. Noting clusters of people gathered at various corners, he guessed that these might be bus stops. He chose one direction that seemed to head up a long avenue stretching to the north and decided to practice his recently acquired skill and habit of taking chances.

Fingering the few coins the ship staff had sold him, and a tiny slip of paper, he boarded the first bus that pulled over. For four years he had carefully kept the paper; he now pulled it from his pocket and handed it silently to the driver with a couple of coins. The man patiently looked at the writing on the paper, handed it back to José, along with one of the coins, and motioned to him to sit down in the seat opposite that provided a full view of the driver. When the bus lurched forward, José cranked his head from side to side, peering out windows and marveling at the height of the buildings that lined the avenue—taller than he had ever imagined possible. It seemed as if the bus and its occupants moved through a tunnel of concrete for some time when eventually three- and four-story connected buildings, with wide steps in front of each, began to dominate the landscape. After about a dozen stops, the bus pulled over and this time the driver grunted at José and motioned for him to get off.

As the bus pulled away with a groan and puffs of exhaust, he reclaimed the paper from his pocket and peered at the numbers and letters on it. José looked at the corner and saw a sign that matched a number on the paper. He then looked at the building right in front of him and saw, above the doorway at the top of the stairs, another number—and it was on the paper, too! He climbed six or seven stairs and reached the door. Locked! Peering through the glass, he could see a hallway alongside an inside staircase. He not only had to figure out how to get inside, but which door to knock on. But… someone was at that moment coming through the door and stopped, looked inquisitively at him and José heard himself stammer a name at the man, "Shamo Giragossian?"

The man mumbled something and ran back inside and up the stairs, leaving José in the doorway. He waited, perplexed but not anxious. Worry seemed to have evaporated from his body, even as the sweat trickled down his neck, while he stood under an angled late summer sun and contemplated the recent string of miracles.

Within a few minutes he heard rapid footsteps on the stairs, a face in shadow pressed against the glass door which then flew open, a voice was calling, "Hovsep, Hovsep Karamardian!" And there was his uncle in front of him, breathless, embracing him, holding his two tanned cheeks and kissing each one.

"Barev, Hovsep!"

It was all true. He was in Amirka. Nobody and nothing had stopped him.

CHAPTER 9

SALT

New York State - 1909

JOSEPH

The guy on the train said his name was Leo Abraham.

"When does the train arrive at Utica?" José's question initiated a snort from the shorter man. But, as if the man regretted his outburst, it quickly transformed into a kinder tone.

"Sorry, man, the train to Utica goes north to Albany first, then a transfer. This train heads to Binghamton, Ithaca, and Buffalo. You got the wrong one."

Stomach lurching, José frantically forced his mind backward, searching for a clue to his error. Penn Station itself felt like a journey, as impressive and grand as the Paris Gare of his memory. The vast ceilings were endless, the tile flooring amplified echoing footsteps, the sounds of a thousand voices and engines braking on the tracks below bounced through the cavernous space. He had been grateful to find the track, jump into the open car, and breathe in its stale air, sweetly buffered from the deafening noise.

The conversation in Arabic began about two hours after the train pulled out of the station. José correctly guessed the man sitting alone was Syrian, but when he introduced himself he carefully sounded out his Armenian name, and immediately wondered if that had been a wise decision. Many Syrians were traumatized by the risks of engaging with Armenians back home, where punishment from Ottoman officials could descend at anytime. Yet so far, the habit of shunning Armenians was decidedly less pronounced in the countries he had traveled through, including Dominica. He could also distinguish that most immigrant Syrians tended to be Christians who had themselves fled the persecution of Ottomon cruelty.

"Aine Hovsep Bedros Karamardian." He used the Arabic verb for *I am.*

"Can you write it?" Leo asked, and Jose wondered what he was getting at.

"Of course. Youssif Boutris. Oh. You mean in English?"

"Yeah. Maybe you…make it simple. The boys from Melkia… normally we take our father's first name as our surname. In the Orthodox tradition, we are introduced that way. Now that we live here, we keep the same name for our children. You can do that, too. What is your father's name?"

"Bedros. Boutris."

Leo knew some English and could translate names.

"If you need work, come to the salt block with me. Another local train will take us up the lake to Myers. Tell them you are *Josef Peter*. That will work fine."

Josef. That part was easy. He had been using similar versions of his name all along. Plus, he had heard this English name from the missionaries, and Walter. Boutris was an easy name, too, José thought for about five minutes. He thought about his journey this far. He thought about his father whose name he was inserting into a new world. Lastly, he thought about where he was headed. Having no specific promise of employment in Utica, beyond some general information about factory work and Middle Eastern communities, he decided to waste no emotion lamenting his mistake. With a shrug, he even wondered if perhaps he was blessed with luck. It was mid-March and the air in the train car felt full of promise.

After the two men changed trains at the Ithaca depot, the second ride took no more than twenty minutes to the place along the lakefront. As the slow-moving train screeched to a full stop, Josef counted several tall well towers and over nine buildings. It looked so modern and large, this sprawling operation between the railroad track and the water's edge, and when he turned his gaze to the other side of the train car, he could see it spilled over onto that side of the tracks, too. As they stepped down to the landing that faced the main building, the smell of salt overwhelmed him instantly. The supervisor looked at him keenly, having noticed his height to be a couple of inches higher than the small Syrian workers. He wrote down his name, the English version as "Joseph Peter" and asked, "Language?"

Puzzled, Joseph began rattling off his tongues without translating them to English. "Armenian, Turkish, Syrian Arabic, French, Spanish...?"

The man lifted his head from the clipboard and squinted at him.

"Arabic, you say? Syrian?"

"*No, Armenian, but I born in Syria so talk all language from tere.*" Joseph's English was barely conversational, and he could not pronounce a 'th' combination, but Mr. McGuire seemed impressed with him anyway.

"Okay. You will be in charge of the group at boiler six. The men are all from one town. Now for lodging, let's see..." He flipped through some pages and jabbed his pencil at the lists. "Aha! You will stay in dwelling #159, group 164. Jacob, Manas, and Manas. Add Peter..."

"*Don't put me with tose guys! I want learn more better English.*"

"Sorry. Head over and introduce yourself." McGuire dismissively pointed in the direction of the main building behind him that stood long and narrow, perpendicular to the tracks. It was that simple.

Stepping into the main building he could immediately make out four connecting rooms. The mill and the pan rooms were three stories high. The other two rooms of one level each included the unmistakable roar of an engine room and a boiler room which held twelve Fitz-gibbons 250 horsepower boilers. The fact that he had no clue how to operate these impressive machines held little relevance for him. He rolled up his sleeves as he strolled over to boiler number six and introduced himself in Syrian, then stood aside to watch the men for a while. Silent glares flew over shoulders and looks passed among them with open faces of disgust. Joseph kept silent, pretending to inspect their work until he could catch on to the process. He knew he must jump in beside them, work faster and longer, and prove himself in time. Some of them acted like they were pouting, and he overheard more than a few mutter, "God damned Armine," and "How dare he boss us!" He was neither surprised nor bothered.

"I do my job, tey do teirs. We get used to each other," he practiced thinking such thoughts to himself in English, determined to use every moment constructively.

Gratefully, Joseph was not to be housed with the Syrians who resented him. When he entered the free-standing house along the railroad tracks he was pleasantly surprised, shocked actually, to meet his housemates. In a surreal daze, he walked into the house and heard his native language, Armenian; though not his Kessabtsi dialect, it was certainly an unimaginable treat after the long inaugural day of work!

The Manas brothers were so far apart in age they were more like father and son; Shin was seventeen and Samuel was thirty-five. They had come from near Beyruth (Beirut), and like Joseph, had lived among Arabic peoples, though with less command of the Syrian language. They had shortened their surnames: Manassian to Manas, which easily passed as their father's first name to the Syrian workers with whom they were surrounded at work. Everyone fit in better that way and none of them could have spelled their Armenian names anyway. Poor Ann Jacob had made a stab at translation and ended up with a girl's name through some clerk's error that would one day be fixed. Joseph mercifully called him Armen. The guys were okay, the card games at night a welcome release, and at times it was almost like evenings back home. As far as Joseph could tell, they were the only four Armenians around this region, bunked together barrack style in the second-floor loft bedroom that could get quite hot at night.

The street snaked from the International Salt Company on the flats, along railroad tracks that stretched along the lake's edge, to a park where the land spit out into the water on either side of Salmon Creek. At the southern end, the road swerved away up a hill and made way to several small farms. But in front of the park, rows of clapboard houses lined up so close to one another you could hear snoring through the two walls that separated them. The morning train, only yards from the houses, shook the walls no matter how slowly it moved along the track through the trestle bridge behind them. Most of the houses were owned or rented by some of the older laborers and housed from two to five boarders, in addition to wives and children living there. Two larger houses above the park were occupied by some rich families who came only in summers. These had gardens and indoor plumbing.

The street that wound beside the tracks was noisy and vibrant, reminding Joseph of the energetic city life he had known in Ladehkiya, Santo Domingo, and Noo York, but without the density of the sound and volume of human bodies. The loudest sound, besides the train, came from the creek in spring when the snows melted; it roared like a waterfall. At dusk, he would typically join the guys clustered on the creek bridge for a smoke, aware that the young girls stayed conspicuously away. These gatherings stretched past sunset in the summer months and, as the sun extended its influence into warmer nights, so too did the lengthy games of cards at someone's house after its disappearance.

By spring of 1909, Joseph knew all of his immediate neighbors on both sides of Salmon Creek, Syrians and some Hungarians. He tried to meet the Americans too, some of whom farmed small plots of land with only their wives and perhaps, a boarder who was also the only laborer. He envied them their lives but knew their enterprises were too small to take on further employees. On one side of the creek was a group of young couples, along with the widow Arvilla Love and the Muck family; on the other side were Swedish engineer John Johnson and family, the Whitlat family (Milton and Lizzie), and the dressmaker Ray Norris and wife, Noella.

That Christmas Eve, Joseph's second Christmas in America, the people of the community came together on the street. He heard it first. From outside of the house, a beautiful wall of sound lured the Armenians out the door. They followed the singing and found the gathering near the intersection of the road and the park entrance, in front of a little store owned by the young couple, Leo and May Emmons: Americans, Swedes, Hungarians, Syrians, even foreman Will McGuire and his pregnant wife, filled the street. Joe saw his first friend, Leo Abraham, with his Flora. He saw the Isaacs, the Nickolases, Charles and Daniel George with their two other brothers. There was Shas Soloman, Sarah and Dan Mike and George Moses. Everyone from the salt block was there, along with the farmers and the rest of the people of the community.

The carols were in American, but Joseph had heard some of them before, at the mission schools in Kessab as a boy and in Ladehkiya as an adolescent and teen, where his teachers had been Presbyterians. He heard himself humming familiar melodies into the cold air. Shin and Samuel looked at him, amazed that he could keep up with the American tunes, even though he managed only a few sporadic words. He explained it to them in Armenian, not wishing to attract attention among the Syrians. But someone had noticed.

A very tall man pushed his way through the bodies to stand next to Joseph.

"Are you Armine? I couldn't help but overhear. Please forgive me, but you speak a dialect I recognize. Are you from Syria?" The man's Arabic was formal and educated. "I am Eassa Hanna Simon."

"Yes, I come from Ladehkiya, born in Kessab." Joseph tried to speak as accurately as he had been taught in school, punching out the consonants, Syrian style.

"I knew it! I am—we are, my family here—we are from Lat-takia." He pronounced the city with an Arabic dialect that sounded like two *ts* clicking together. "I was trained for teaching at the American Mission School. You see, I recognize the Kistinok dialect of Kessab, it is so unique. I have heard it spoken among students at the Mission. We are only recently reunited here at Myers."

Joseph gaped at this John Simon, trying to recall if he had encountered him at school, when a teen, perhaps. Before he could further react, Eassa Simon (Mr. Simon) was calling his family over while the singing continued. The Manas brothers could not easily follow the conversation, and backed away to make room for the summoned boys who began to fill the space around them.

"This is Ameen, my oldest. He came first, in 1905. And my sons Anees and Nageeb, my wife Mary. This is Abraham and Louise. I arrived only this year along with these young ones, Lulu and Nadeen." His hands rested on the shoulders of the children whose names he said last. Each of the brothers leaned forward to politely shake hands with Joseph.

"I am Hovsep. Ibn (son of) Bedros Karamardian, shoemaker in Lattakia. But here I use just the names, Joseph Peter. My friends are…" When he remembered to introduce his housemates, he looked around for them and saw that Shin and Samuel had disappeared into the crowd and his voice faded off.

"Hovsep…Youssef, please. You must come for Christmas dinner." From the start, the Simons automatically referred to his name in Arabic, without thinking.

The community lingered around the store after the singing. Joseph thought this night was the finest he had yet enjoyed in America as he accompanied the Simon family to their home by the bridge. There was much to talk about with the Simons, but it was not all welcome news. Eassa Simon informed him of big troubles just that year: Kessab had been attacked by Turkish rebels from the north and most of the town lost. Though Eassa John Simon was teaching elsewhere at the time, he had been directly involved with helping the missionaries distribute aid to Kessab refugees, most of whom had made it to the Lattakia Mission.

"Even the Lattakia mission school had to temporarily close, as happened in the 90s, from cautionary concern for the occupants, in case of being targeted. The Kessab schools were destroyed. All of them."

Joseph groaned and wondered if his sisters were adapting. He decided in that moment that it was time to write home, if possible. His brothers might be anxious to emigrate. And family in Kessab… He pushed further thoughts away, all useless.

"Eassa Simon, would you be able to help me post a letter?"

The Christian Christmas holiday in Syria and Greece is formally celebrated on January 6th, the custom both Orthodox and Armenian, and Joseph joined the Simon family again on that day for a meal and cheer. It turned out, John Simon taught English to Syrian workers, among other things. Joseph had no patience for a classroom but filed away the information in his head for future reference. He also took a closer look at Najeeb, whose face was vaguely familiar. Perhaps, he thought, he had encountered the boy in the old country. Anything seemed possible in Amirka. His curiosity was noted and rewarded.

"You may have met him, Youssef! Nageeb and Abraham both studied at the mission school." Perhaps brother Manas was in school with them, thought Joseph, and dropped it.

By spring Joseph was reeling in confidence. He learned from McGuire that it was possible to buy the house and be a landlord rather than a tenant, earning small rents on his investment. The payment of rent to another person was galling to Joseph, it just made no sense to throw away hard earned money. He saw owning his home as a way to save for the future, if the price was right. Joseph spent little of his earnings, and he almost had enough saved. He established a goal to buy at summer's end and budgeted his card playing with humor.

His old friend Leo Abraham teased him mercilessly, "Pinochle, Youssif? Or will it stifle your plans to become land baron of Myers?"

By September, when a census taker came to the door asking questions, Joseph proudly announced that he was the homeowner of the laborers' boarding house and rattled off the names of the occupants—now his tenants! Since he had been doing repairs all along, there was little adjustment to the new responsibilities of homeownership. He rebuilt the outhouse with the help of his neighbor John Muck, a carpenter, who taught him to measure in American inches. On Christmas he comfortably joined his American neighbors in front of the corner store for singing and, once again, gratefully rejoined the Simon family for Christmas dinner.

Najeeb owned and played an oud and so, after the plates were collected and chairs pushed back, Syrian folk songs filled the house and more neighbors stopped by. Joseph looked around at the table and thought of how every member of this family, typical to all families of this community, worked at the salt block. Even Louise, still a teenager, worked the salt house with other women. Mother Mary Simon worked the mess hall where all workers ate together at noon for the thirty minute lunch time. Only a few Tubbha residents did not eat with the others, but walked up Syrian Hill to lunch at home. The two youngest Simons, still children, attended school rather than work the ten-hour day shifts of the others.

"You've really accomplished something this year," Eassa Simon was addressing him. "What will be next?"

Returning to the present moment, Joseph considered the question. Rarely, since leaving Syria, had he spent more than a year at any one community or occupation; this stemmed more from necessity than from boredom. Now twenty-two, his life felt different. He had arrived somewhere intentionally, rather than on his way to somewhere else. He thought he was experiencing some level of contentment but wasn't sure what to make of it.

In February, a young man stepped off the Lehigh Valley train and asked for him in Syrian, but using his Armenian name. This caused some confusion. Ultimately, it was Tony Isaac who sorted it out.

"Bete, Bete Armine. Youssif! Come to the platform! There is someone here for you."

Joseph's heartbeat sped up with excitement, not knowing who to expect. A cousin? A friend from New York? He tried to walk normally through the snow piles and past the bagging house where the girls and women worked. Arriving near the half dozen halted train cars, he shaded his eyes against the overhead sun and glistening snow but could not make out the figure until he was face to face with grey eyes beaming back at him.

"Khatchig? Barev!! I did not know…." he gasped, all other words eluding him. The brothers held each other for some minutes then pulled apart to slap the backs they had just clutched.

"When did you dock? How did you find your way to the salt block?"

"Oh, Hovsep, such a winding story. I've been to Greece and back—twice!" Khatchig was laughing now, but he was not to stay long. He had only wanted to find his big brother before making his way to Detroit. He had a contact there and had been told about plenty of work making the famous automobiles. This was new information for Joseph. For three long nights of talking, smoking, playing cards, and sometimes just staring at one another, the brothers shared some, but not all, that had happened since they were last together. Khatchig's journey was nothing like the one that Joseph and his older brother had experienced six years earlier.

"It took me three weeks to get to Greece. I had to go through Aleppo and all of Turkey by erratic train schedule, nervous all the way. I was so mad, when I arrived I threw my fez disguise away!"

"But you managed to get passage?"

"Yes, on the *Laura*. The crew plays cards. They invite you to join them if you hang around."

"Yah, I did that too, on every boat!"

"But Hovsep, this Greek crew has a scam going. They won all my money. I was broke and when we docked, the authorities told me I couldn't disembark without any money."

"What happened?"

"They held me in a hold for two days, locked up on the *Laura*! I could not leave the ship, or even come on deck. Then they put me on another freighter, the *SS Oceana*, that sailed all the way back to Patras!"

"How did you get another passage to return on the new ship?"

"The same way! The *Oceana* had a good card game going and a mixed crew, not just Greeks. I played all across the Atlantic back to Greece, and this time I won enough money to pay for the return passage."

"And did you lose any on the return to New York?"

"Are you kidding? I stopped playing, took no chances!" The Karamardian brothers roared with laughter and slammed their cards down on the table. The Manas brothers laughed just as loudly and called the next hand.

Not a word had been spoken yet of the troubles from the year and few months before, that Eassa Simon said had befallen the Kessab people. Joseph hesitated about whether to bring it up. But finally, before they slept, he asked if the family had suffered.

"Hovsep, most of the people of Kessab walked to Ladehkiya! One priest from Kessab led many of them. Uncle Asadour and his family stayed in our home for awhile after the Turks drifted away. Their house was left a pile of rubble. The family shoe shops of Kessab were all destroyed. Everything was changed then. Hayrig began talking to me and Manas about following you here. It felt very surprising, but by that point, staying seemed impossible, even to him. Nishan will one day take over the shop, but the shop cannot possibly sustain all of us. Even Hayrig stated what is obvious to all. 'We have no future in the Ottomon world.'" Then Khatchig's face lit up. "Did you know that Nishan has already two girls and a boy?"

When Khatchig teased Joseph about his new identity, "From Hovsep to Joh-zef," Joseph retorted, "You left out the half of it! I was also José (Hozay) and Youssef. The Syrians call me Bete, too." And it was Joseph's turn to tease.

"You'll see. I wonder what your name will become."

Joseph accompanied Khatchig on the Saturday train to the Ithaca depot and the brothers again held each other.

"Hovsep, come to Detroit. I'll write when I settle, if things are good there, who knows?"

"Who knows…" And before Khatchig parted, Joseph asked about word from Asadour.

"Hovsep, we have heard nothing! Not since you were together on that island. But I think perhaps you will see Manas. Maybe he has received word since I left. He spoke of little else than of leaving Ladehkiya, so I am surprised he did not arrive before me!"

It was just six months later that Manas arrived, at the end of August. He had traveled with the boys' cousins Boghos and Asadour of Giragos, who were on their way to study in Rochester, New York. In Auburn, Manas found and boarded the Black Diamond that brought him down the lake to the salt works. Two brothers in six months! If emotions were gathering in Joseph, he had no time to contemplate or acknowledge them. Life moved fast enough, and he liked it that way.

However, Joseph discovered it a challenge to talk his foreman into taking on the small, wiry figure that was his youngest brother. Finally, McGuire agreed to place the kid on the slide crew, which required a lot of shoveling. Modeling himself after Joseph and all the Syrian boys, Manas reinvented himself as Leo Peter. For his part, Joseph was ever more thankful he had bought the house, in order to provide Leo with lodging. But he was also mindful of Leo's impulsive and sometimes volatile nature; he stayed vigilant to prevent disharmony among his housemates. The year 1911, with two surprises already, was not yet over.

International Salt Company Loading dock circa 1910
Photo courtesy of Lansing Historical Society

INTERLUDE

$\mathcal{A}$RMENIANS
Ithaca - 1965

AUTHOR

The day after Jido's funeral, life resumed and I returned to school. Aunt Ruth's words still haunted me, "The Turks killed Jido's family..." Without a clue as to their meaning, I nonetheless felt primed, hyper alert and sensitive to any related thought. My seventh-grade social studies class was on the second floor in the farthest corner of the building, directly over the cafeteria and the escaping aromas of lunch preparation that triggered everyone's impatience for lunch period. I sat at a metal desk in the second row, two thirds of the way back, while the teacher introduced a new unit on civil rights. I do not remember his name or face, but the message permeated my pores.

I stared down at the desk, at an open book there. The printed words blurred as the teacher spoke of injustices that inflamed my imagination. Very slowly, the things that were being discussed floated into focus, clearer and clearer, until the stunning moment of comprehension flashed at me from the shiny surface it had arrived at: these events were happening in real time! I tried to wrap my head around what real people were experiencing as I sat there—real people with dark skin color, in southern states. People were being banned from certain buildings, bathrooms, school rooms, stores... People were beaten for breaking such rules. Some defied them at great cost. How can human beings be subjected to such rules? That such mistreatment and crimes against human beings could be happening in our own country!

Suddenly nothing was right with the world. Jido was gone; he was not Syrian after all; I no longer knew exactly who my tribe was. And now, a theft of innocence—swiping at my basic faith in goodness—had turned everything inside out in the course of one forty-minute class session.

After the last bell of the school day, I raced the few blocks to the county public library on State Street. Our upstate New York college town was very compact. The downtown area was unlike the Cornell campus which sprawled all over the hill to the east. DeWitt Junior High was only two blocks from the library. I had plenty of time and one intention: to look up the one word that had taken lodging in my brain. The librarian was elderly and very sweet. I sounded out the word: *Armenian.*

"What kind of information are you needing, dear?" she patiently asked.

"I don't know," I stammered. I was ashamed to admit that I didn't know what the word meant. Was it a country? No, I didn't think so, because Jido came from Syria. That much I knew for sure. Was it a race? I had not asked my family, nor did I yet wonder why the information had escaped me. Surely, my parents and older siblings knew about it. Perhaps, I was merely ashamed of my ignorance. Maybe I'd not yet had any experience with the emotion of shame.

She directed me to a history section and pulled out some books with sections on countries. Ancient history and the like. I read about the Armenian peoples and something about their tragic history, presumably ancient news. From the few books opened on the table, I read words and paragraphs about things done to my grandfather's people. Could this have happened to his very own family, people we knew nothing about? It felt personal.

A vague, incomprehensible rage began to germinate and co-mingle with the disturbing discoveries that day in social studies class—two exposures to the cruelty that lives in humankind. I had stared with glassy eyes into an open book throughout the Jim Crow discussion while the dawning realization that human life can be so vulnerable crushed my soul. Now the vague words in front of me about the Armenian "people" offered a sense of things that may have happened to the unnamed ancestors whose existence I had just been made aware of, only twenty-four hours earlier. Somehow, this felt further away, faded by both time and distance, while racial segregation was happening in real time in my own country. Confused is an overused word, but it was the only one that can adequately characterize my state of mind at the end of that impactful day.

I don't know who told me about the book. Such a life-changing event should jump to mind. But the impact when I devoured it set the tone for a journey that would consume my life. Franz Werfel's *Forty Days of Musa Dagh* was my first vivid introduction to the events of 1915, when more than 1.5 million Armenians were killed by an Ottoman government intent on cleansing the empire of its most influential minority population. I was not yet aware that this classic tale of resilience and defiance was a true story which actually took place at the village closest to, and a mountain away from, our family hometown of Kessab. The men of Musa Dagh defied the Ottoman authorities' order to relinquish any weapons and instead, stockpiled all the munitions they could gather. When news of the systematic raids on Armenian villages, followed by forced marches of women and children, reached Musa Dagh, its people climbed up the mountain and fought valiantly against the Turkish unit that came for them. Miraculously, a French ship appeared off the coast and rescued those few who survived the battle and reached the shore. The rescued were taken to safety in Egypt for the duration of the war. It appears that throughout the Ottomon Empire's assault on its Armenian minorities, only four communities resisted the Turks and, sadly, the only triumphant story is that of Musa Dagh. I was intrigued to learn that MGM studios in Hollywood had picked up the rights in 1934 and was in full production of making a movie of the Musa Dagh story when the U.S. government, under pressure from the Turkish government, emphatically shut it down. Major American movie studios spent another 48 years trying to film the Werfel novel with constant "international obstacles."

The learning that began that afternoon at the Tompkins County Library was followed by reading everything that crept into my new Armenian awareness, new books for every decade. The 'Armenian story' is the theme of most everything written about, or by, Armenians. It typically refers to the 1915 Genocide. It should not be controversial as it is a documented fact, witnessed by the entire first-generation of Armenian immigrants around the diaspora, as well as aid workers and diplomats in the region at that time. Turkey still denies it and makes it a crime to mention the word 'genocide.' And for more than a century Turkey managed to influence the United States—my own country—to kill every legislative vote that brought to the floors of Congress a bill to officially recognize the April 24th as the anniversary of the Genocide. The majority of the rest of the world has long since taken that step, made that minimal gesture toward a people for their unimaginable suffering during a time when the world, distracted by the first big war, turned its back (and made it possible for history to repeat itself during the next war). I eventually learned, through the writings of Peter Balakian (*The Black Dog of Fate*), that the refusal of Turkey to recognize history and its government's continuous efforts to subvert education of the subject, which includes the purchasing of library seats within American universities, is still living history.

We called these topics "current events" when I was a teenager. It seems to me, those issues appear to still be alive and kicking—from civil rights to Holocaust deniers to Turkish denial of Armenian history--well over a century later. When I learned that Jido was Armenian, I was as ignorant as most Americans in the 1960s, as well as today, who have never been taught about the first major genocide of the 20th century. It was not only missing in school curricula, few teachers have known anything about it.

Even Aunt Laura described a time when she was curious about her father's heritage and asked for the name of a book that would give her information about the Genocide. It was 1944 and the high school history teacher she called Old Lady Watkins, snarled at her, "No such thing ever happened!"

I was about fifteen, when Michael Arlen's *Passage to Ararat* spoke to the identity crises woven into the natural drama of a full-blown teenager and deepened the tone for my journey to come. It introduced me to questions that would haunt for a lifetime. In his own search for identity, Arlen described a certain Armenian quality he observed in the first-generation Armenians of his father's age. A sort of victimhood that went one of two ways: the horrors that survivors of that generation endured became something to either lock up or to bemoan ceaselessly. It confused him. His own father (also named Michael Arlen) never spoke a word of Armenian things, and yet was often surrounded by Armenian people who spoke of it endlessly.

The questions Arlen posed are ones he himself had sought answers to, and they spoke directly to my heart: What was this feeling Armenians carried around like ghosts of the past? Why were they silent about it (as was Jido)? Or, always openly mourning (as in books I had begun to devour)? These expressions of the Armenians around Arlen, like generational PTSD, are also commonly discussed in terms of Holocaust survivors and their families. What Arlen described came to be known in later decades as ancestral trauma. It did not seep into my family history through any sort of communication. I was raised in a town with many ethnic groups but only one silent Armenian: my Jido, who never spoke of his past. Ancestors were lost to me, to us. There was so little: a name of a town, snippets of kidnapped aunts and lost brothers that lit my imagination but were too vague to grasp, like a collage of magazine cut-outs that don't fit together into an actual puzzle. Any of what Dad and his siblings knew of their father came from their mother. My grandmother, called Sito, was the storyteller and heartbeat of the family.

I never knew her. The only grandparent in my physical life was Joe Peter—albeit with some lost name—and I thrilled to contemplate that he was the father of my father and all my aunts and uncles. The first time I consciously encountered the vastness of the universe, I was about seven years old, lying on my back in the grass in the Sepulveda's front yard in our Puerto Rican neighborhood and squinting at a blade of the coarse southern grass that I held up toward the sun. Wonder overtook me as the strip of green sparkled in my vision. Vastness, the only word. It's like that when

I think of family. Jido was responsible for the whole tribe that surrounded me, a tribe that gifted me with a sensation that I was part of something larger than me. He was the pulse beneath the whole thing that was my world and I adored him for it.

I naturally adored anything that had to do with him: his life, his past, his secrets. What was his world? Just who was this tribe that cocoons me? After all, it was the choices he made that created the rest of us and all who come after us: a string of choices by each of us—all those random, seemingly arbitrary decisions (what bus shall I take to work today?), those puzzle pieces—are directly responsible for the existence of every living being on the family tree. I knew a bit about my parents' coming together, their story. I needed to understand Jido's choices, any one of which, or all of which, caused me, us, my tribe, to exist. It was all so…VAST.

"He chose a random bus to board and showed his piece of paper with an address scrawled on it to the bus driver. The driver motioned him to sit down. Eventually, the driver motioned him to get off at a certain stop, and when he stepped off the bus he realized the building in front of him was the one on the paper! Pa worked in the city (New York) for five or six months, at some factory. He made five dollars a week." Uncle John told me all of this.

"It was a spaghetti factory," Aunt Laura added later when, in her last years, our conversations were more casual and more frequent. "He hated it. He would never eat spaghetti that I can recall. Ma and I used to eat spaghetti only if Pa was away or out of the house." Laura was the youngest child, the only one to live alone with her parents for any years. She, too, recounted, "He had a slip of paper in his pocket, with an address of a cousin or an uncle."

Though little was known of facts, countless anecdotes like these strung together vivid scenes of moments in Jido's life. Enough for me to "see" blurry images and hear his voice, the one that Uncle John often mimicked in the staccato, brittle syllables of his broken accent. Still, I needed to know how he got to those moments. What his world was like from beginning to middle and end. The backstory was limited to a few vague sentences that began with the one uttered at a card table by Aunt Ruth:

"You know, Jido was actually Armenian."

I still didn't know what that meant. But I was idealistic and expectant. And too naïve to harbor any doubt about my mission, floating somewhere in the future beyond my immediate reach.

CHAPTER 10

EDUCATION
Kaladouran - 1911

LOUISA

Could I be any happier? I fear my heart will erupt into a thousand stars if another drop of goodness were to be poured into it. Yesterday, I awoke a schoolgirl, in preparation for advancement to teacher, in the favor of the missionaries—my teachers. By August, I will be teacher at the high school, an honor. A life of joy stretches before me with each morning's short walk to Kessab. It is so blinding that I could not see beyond August and my first days of facing the children, only slightly younger than me, in my new position of sharing knowledge. That was yesterday and it was enough.

Today, I awake even more than a schoolgirl or a teacher. I am blessed and beloved. I am betrothed. I am to marry my Asadour. My neighbor. My beloved. My all.

We spoke of it last night. He was mysterious, as if there were more to say.

"Louisa, my heart, I want nothing more than our marriage. Though it cannot be immediate, the knowledge of it is all I desire for the coming days," he said after proposing our union. "May we speak more after tomorrow? I must prepare for an early morning journey to Ladehkiya with Hayrig, for supplies." His black eyes shine so deeply, at times I cannot read them. They glisten in depths that seem to range in possibility from profound joy to despair.

I eagerly await his return tomorrow to take up what is on his mind. But today, I feel myself glow. I must be sparkling with the wellbeing I can look forward to. It will be a great moment to share the happiness with Hayrig and Mayrig tonight, though I suspect that by the time I return home to the village, they will know more than me. As will everyone else in the village. Meanwhile, I must redirect thought to the daily lessons, so that I finish the year properly and do not squander my great opportunity. I will be a teacher and a wife to Asadour. Two great missions. My good fortune is not to be taken for granted.

I glance at the sky when I reach the place where the path levels out at Karadash. I look backward, at the vision that always catches my breath from the top of Dapusa Mountain, 990 meters above the sea. Can the world be more glorious than this? It is tempting to linger here and cherish my happiness, but I must not be late. I am halfway to school from our village of Kaladouran; I can hardly wait to meet up with Louise, my best friend and Asadour's sister. We will finish our studies at the end of this month. When we climb Jebel Aqra in August for the Feast of the Virgin Mary, we will walk apart from the families, as proud new graduates. It is a Kessab tradition. And for me, there will be more. I will be among the betrothed, and celebrated for this, too. I wonder if Louise suspects? I will be able to guess at her very first glance, for she is entirely unable to withhold any secret. Enough of dreaming! I force my thoughts to the day's lessons, for there is much yet to finish.

Although our people find value in education, I am well aware that this is not true for all children in our country. My teacher, Miss May, told me this when I turned fifteen.

"You are fortunate to be an Armenian girl, Louisa. If you were an Arabic girl, you would never have even seen the inside of the school, unless to clean it. Even Armenian, were you Catholic or Apostolic, you would likely be married before now and your studies would cease."

Nobody had told me this before, so I could hardly imagine it. Then I thought, I do not know an Arabic girl. Not a single Arabic family lived in Kaladouran, and only one or two in Kessab, so I have never met a girl who is not Armenian. I've seen Arabic women in Ladehkiya, when we travel to visit relatives. But they are clothed so fully that they appear as lumps of cloth carrying baskets, walking through the streets there. I was more curious about this when I was a little girl but have since given little thought to people beyond our schools and villages. We have eight elementary schools in the Kessab region, more than one for each village, filled with boys and girls alike. And the Protestant girls tend to complete their studies, marrying later than the others, according to the missionaries. One more thing to thank God in Heaven for, I add to a mental list that has accumulated more blessings than one girl should be allowed.

I have long known our school was begun in 1849. And Miss May told me that girls' education had been deemed a priority among the mission movement since 1859. It certainly caught on with the other schools of Kessab, too. All in all, there are twenty schools in the region of Kessab, since separate schools are run by the Apostolics and Catholics. This reflects our unique community of three denominations. Good Hope Catholic School began in 1864, almost as old as ours. And School of the Armenian Apostolic Church started in 1848, one year before our Nahadagats Miatsyal Armenian Evangelical School was founded.

The missionaries had been working in Beirut already for twenty years by then, teaching girls at the schools founded by Isaac Bird and William Goodell, and at another school established there by Eliza Thompson and Martha Dodge, in 1834. I have memorized these names, as I am obliged to do, along with that of the missionary wife, Sarah L. Smith, who expanded the school and gained a positive reputation that allowed for the later establishment of a central hub in Kessab and Ladehkiya.

The mission had later established itself in Turkey for the Christian populations, beginning in Aintab in 1874 with sister colleges throughout Anatolia. But one of these, named Turkey College for Girls, was burned in 1890. Some Muslims were supportive, but most were not. I learned, in preparation for a history exam, that by 1896, seven hundred missionaries were teaching throughout the Holy Land. But the first (Armenian) massacres of 1895 affected the school at Aintab, and the recent troubles just two years ago, which reached all the way to Kessab, wiped out more of the schools to the north, around Adana. Gratefully, our people were open from the beginning for girls to learn to read and write, and I feel proud of this fact. Miss May says it is imperative that we continue the tradition of teaching one another and that my intellect is a gift to my community!

"I heard!" Louise is squealing as she races toward me, taking me by surprise. While reviewing my history lesson, I have arrived at the school like a ghost who floats from one place to another. I now realize that Louisa must have walked early to school, since she did not accompany me, and I wonder why. I get my answer.

"I was sure you would come early to town, so I rushed to meet you, but I was wrong. I am so excited, I thought you must be, too. We are to be sisters, two Louisas in one household!" she laughs in the way I love, head thrown back with a throated rumble. Dear, sweet Louise. But I must say I am surprised that Asadour told her before I could. It is not in his nature to reveal news such as this without careful strategy. I love everything about his nature.

Louise is still talking. "Not only will we be sisters, but we will share a whole name!" I cannot help but chuckle. We Armenians are so predictable about names. I, Louisa Guzelian, will join the ranks of others when I become Louisa Karamardian: Asadour's aunt, a cousin, the wife of his cousin, Nishan and, of course, my best friend and soon to be sister-in-law. Four of us with some version of the same name. Just as there are three Asadour Karamardians; one uncle and two cousins. Hah! This is a habit among us. If we continue to pass on names like this within families, there will be no variation. No doubt, I may acquire a new nickname, like the others.

I link my arm through Louise's. "Well, dear sister, let's get in class before the missionaries turn us into something besides Louisas." And the laugh that surges from deep in her belly once more wraps me in its silky joy and creeps into my soul.

My favorite part of the day comes after the lessons, when I help with the children at the elementary school. Miss May had arranged it and I spent a few hours every afternoon preparing games that fool the youngest school-aged children into believing they are playing, while they are actually learning basic skills like arithmetic and language. I should never admit favorites, not ever. But I cannot suppress the love I feel for little Elisa Karamardian, one of Asadour's littlest cousins. She is as sharp-minded as she is personable. Today her face is bright and her voice breathless as she stumbles near.

"Vahan is talking, Louisa! My little brother speaks! I am a teacher, already!" Elisa announced to me in recent days that she wishes to be a teacher when she grows up, like me.

"Elis-jan, that is amazing. You are amazing! What are his first words?"

"He said Eh..yeez. For Elisa, me! I will teach him more today," she giggles with joy.

Later, that day, I share my happiness at home. Hayrig responds in a philosophical manner, which is one of the things I so love about him.

"You are indeed a lucky girl, Louisa, that your Asadour has not departed like most of the young men of Kessab. There is so little to keep them here since the troubles. Already, Asadour's cousin Khatchig has left Ladehkiya, following his older brothers."

He refers, of course, to the massacre two years ago. April 23rd, it was. Some thirty thousand Turkish men, not soldiers actually, more like rogue militia, descended from Antioch and set fire to the villages north of Kessab. Everyone from town went scrambling into the mountains while some of the young boys stood ground to give cover. I raced the four kilometers from school to Kaladouran. My heart pounded up the mountain and still felt close to bursting as I descended into the valley, screaming to my parents to take cover. We harnessed a cart and headed south. On the road to Ladehkiya, we met up with other townspeople, some with carts, most on foot. Father Sabattino, of the monastery in town, led us all to Basit on the coast, halfway to the city. We waited there, as he rode a donkey on to Ladehkiya to find us some help. My hayrig shook his head and muttered, "Those boys will pay with their lives, so we could make it this far." The boys who stayed back, they were mostly teenaged—some were my schoolmates—and armed only with their shifteh hunting rifles.

Then the ships came, two French ships. At the harbor, we clamored into the boat that had the name *Niger* painted on its stern. It was not far to go, but I'll never know if we could have made it on foot, or if the Turks would have followed and killed us. In Ladehkiya, the Latin monasteries and missions gave us shelter. Asadour and Louisa's family went to stay with their Uncle Bedros in the city's Armenian quarter, along with some other Karamardian cousins. My neighbor, Asadour's cousin Shoushan, was with us at the mission, along with her family. We Guzelians were mostly housed with other families of our village: Ghazarians, Manjikians, Titizians, Saghdejians… We made makeshift beds on the floors of classrooms and tearooms.

I shudder to recall those long, fearsome days. Although we felt safe in the big city, we had no idea for how long we must remain and what we would find back home. My thoughts remained with the boys. So many rumors swirled through the dark dormitories where we lay on pallets through sleepless nights. Some said that most of the Kessab boys had remained, others said only a handful. It turned out that three hundred boys and men fought the Turks that poured down the slopes of Jebel Aqra, so we residents could escape. Of those, 160—more than half—did not survive their bravery.

We returned in about three weeks, after a British battleship arrived off our village coast and scared the attackers away, back to Antioch. The teachers call the event Adana Massacre, for the city in which it began and where few of our people survived. And they say that we must learn from 1909 and remain vigilant at all times. They do not trust the new Ottoman government—these "Young Turks"—that have overthrown the sultan in Constantinople.

We are still rebuilding most of Kessab. Our home in Kaladouran has recovered, but the town's center was mostly destroyed, and the school was in terrible shape. But many organizations are helping with costs and materials and aid to those who were left without shelter when we returned. Even the Turkish government is aiding with the rebuild. Hayrig says they are pretending the attackers were not associated with the official military, yet how could they have created so much damage and killing from Antioch to Kessab without somebody looking the other way? It saddens me to take on cynical thoughts. I know it is against my nature. Yet I must learn all I can from my elders and respect their instincts along with the wisdom they have earned.

I rise to clear the plates from the table just as Shoushan steps inside the door. She often does so after supper; it is her little moment of relaxation, she says, from her ongoing daily work and a break from her small children. Her husband, Shamo, gives her thirty minutes of time while he plays with the small children. Their oldest, Frieda, will be my student in the fall. I am thinking of this when Shoushan shares some news.

"Some of the boys will leave to Amirka in two months. They will study at university," she says proudly. I suspect she must know of whom she is speaking, so I ask.

"Hmmm, Churukian, I believe, Boghossian… that is all I recall."

Asadour has a Boghossian cousin, named Boghos. I wonder if it is he. His father works for a rich man in Ladehkiya.

"Which Amirka?" asks my mother. Most of the boys go to the southern continent, Sao Paulo or Buenos Aires. I have learned about the cities in school.

"A place called *Noo York*, I think," says Shoushan. "Wherever that is." But I know it is in the north.

Asadour doesn't come home until Saturday. It surprised me that he and his father Giragos spent an extra two days in the city, away from the shoe shop. Typically, they stay at his Uncle Bedros' and spend a day purchasing leather goods, but this was unusual. I am especially surprised when he comments, "No, Louisa-jan, Hayrig came home on Thursday. I remained behind with cousin Boghos." Something lurches in my stomach. There is no reason, I tell myself, but nonetheless, I feel the same queasiness of the stomach as when I've had too much lamb. I must shake it loose, remain calm and present.

"I'm so glad you're home, Asadour. I missed you, of course, but I also hope to discuss with you a celebration for us... around the time of Surp Asdvadzadzin—" But he puts a finger on my lips. The touch of his finger causes me to melt into a tender place and, at the same time I feel the unease return and creep back up my legs to my stomach.

"Louisa, my love, we must talk. It is possible—no, quite likely—that I will not be in attendance this year at the Feast of Mary." There it is. It had reached my heart already; pinching, not wanting to hear the words that were to follow, I suck in air. Asadour notices and takes both my hands in his. He leads me to a stone boulder under the grape arbor that connects his family garden with the Merserlians, and gently pushes me under it and onto the solitary stone.

"The reason I stayed in Ladehkiya... well, I don't know where to begin. But Louisa, I have been blessed with an opportunity that I can barely digest. I am still pinching myself."

"You are going to Amirka," I state it flatly, not intending to be cruel, but incapable of mustering enthusiasm even as I pray to be wrong, so wrong.... Asadour gapes at me in disbelief.

"How did you…"

"It's true, then?" I am almost crying now, from inside, trying to keep my voice steady.

"You see, Boghos… His father's employer offered to send him to university, this is how it all began. There was a meeting at an office. And the Churukian brothers are going also, to study medicine. And one other…" The statements string together without sense. I hold in my breath while I wait for the words spilling out of Asadour's mouth to come around to… to where he, Asadour, is involved.

"They arranged it. The steamship, a berth for six men. There are four only. It was decided by our fathers that I will accompany the group and enroll in studies with them. Cousin Manas will travel with us and complete the berth." His sentences burst from his throat, breathlessly. He wants to get it over with, I realize. Then he abruptly stops.

I, too, remain as still as a frightened frog. It takes almost a minute before I feel the tears slipping. Asadour sees them, of course. How could he not? His fingers wipe away a few of them, then he is suddenly kissing the wet tears on the other side of my face! I jerk back instantly, in case someone might see. We are alone, unchaperoned, and my terror is instinctive.

"Louisa-jan, I know you are hurt. But it is for our future! Either I will return more than a shoemaker and make a good life here, or I will return only to collect you. If it is good there, we will make a life in Amirka."

CHAPTER 11

HALOUN

Myers Salt Block - 1911

JOE (A.K.A. JOSEPH/YUSSIF/ BETE)

The first time he saw her, she was under a bag of salt. She was so tiny and bent forward, the heavy ten-pound bag hoisted on her back and shoulder. He might not have taken notice but the sight of a woman almost invisible under the bag grabbed his attention, especially the way she discharged it from over her right shoulder with gusto and a loud plop onto the platform outside the bagging house. She straightened her torso and wiped her brow as she exhaled and lifted her chin to the sky for a moment, then lowered her face and, with a jolt, saw him watching her. She snapped her head away from his gaze and marched back toward the women's house with a proud gait. He wasn't sure, but he almost thought she stomped. What an impervious, extraordinary girl, he thought.

He saw her again at the end of the women's shift; the girls trudged in groups up the hill from the plant, away from the family and men's lodges below on the flats, to the family homes above the cliff on Tubbha Hill. She was all of four feet and maybe ten inches tall, not even one and half meters. Her hair, pulled back on her neck, was auburn, and when it caught the light of the setting sun, Joe imagined it the same hue as the henna color the women used back home, though not as vibrant as his sister Mary's hair. He enjoyed watching her in the days to come and learned her name: Haloun.

When he asked Leo Abraham about her, Leo looked at him askance and narrowed his eyes.

"Youssif, don't mess there. Her brother is Mussa Moses. Our boys from Melkia will not stand for it. Your chances are better with even an American girl than one of their own."

This only made Joe more curious, but he bided his time for a month or so. He didn't speak one word of it, especially to his brother Manas, called Leo by the Syrians, who, he suspected, couldn't be trusted with a secret. It had been five years since he was in any proximity to an Armenian woman and no wonder, he now thought, he was not put off by his attraction to an *odar*. It was astonishing to him that she was a bag carrier when some of the girls inside the salt house filling bags were twice her height and most were heftier. He loved snatching glances her way and observing her energy. Something in her face, the way she thrust her chin forward under the weight of the salt and how she seemed grounded—fearless even—interested him.

By summer she was planted in his head like a continuous melody. He hit upon an idea, a path to approach her. Eassa John Simon held classes after the shift on Saturdays for recent arrivals to get a leg up on speaking English. Normally, Joe would have no patience to attend class and work at a pace determined by others. When he learned Haloun was attending, it occurred to him to take a chance. In summertime, the class met in a makeshift outdoor classroom just outside the salt house. Eassa Simon flashed a quizzical look at Joe when he slipped into earshot and sat right down at the perimeter of the group circle, one knee pulled to his chest, the other leg stretched in front.

"Welcome, Joe. I see you have chosen to expand your skill with the English language."

At first Joe slumped and wished he could sink into the floor. Suddenly the opportunity to show off appeared so obvious, he heard himself speak before realizing he was thinking it.

"Yes, Effendi, thank you. Yes, Eassa, sir. I have been asked by the men in my charge to accompany them to government offices for applications and decided to improve as best I can." After his bumbling address of Eassa Simon, Joe slowed and deliberately spoke the Arabic, as clearly and educated as possible to make an impression on the tiny Syrian girl who Mr. Simon addressed in class as Helen.

Haloun. Helen. The sound reminded him of a bird. She pretended to ignore him, but he caught her glance toward him more than once, then furiously swung her head back to center when he met her eyes. Joe smiled to himself and plotted the next move. He would need to be careful. Any blatant approach would place them both under insurmountable scrutiny and he might get nowhere with her.

On Sundays many of the community enjoyed the park at the water's edge. Picnics were carried down in baskets from Tubbha (the community of eleven houses atop the cliff was known as Syrian Hill) by the women, and the men played baseball and bathed in the lake. Wealthier residents of the greater town of Lansing and some managers at the mine kept wooden boats with single masts and sails docked at the south end of the park. Some workers took the little train along the lake into Ithaca for their free day, either to disembark at Renwick Park to hear the band play or continue to the depot in the west end of town and visit friends living nearby. Joe typically visited the Simon home for Mary Simon's Sunday meal or played cards with Leo and the men near the creek bridge, and occasionally took a stroll through the park at sunset, nodding to acquaintances. But as of July, he lurked most Sundays over by the water, hoping to catch glimpses of, and eventually exchange a word with, Helen Moses.

She often descended the hill with her brother Moses, or a young couple with a baby of one year. They were Abraham and Alice Mahool, with whom Helen boarded. Alice was American. Joe had not yet met a mixed Syrian and American couple and was curious about them beyond their connection to Helen. He made a point to start a conversation with Abe at the beach by asking him what crew he worked with.

Abe was talkative in Syrian and let it be known he cut hair on the side. Joe quickly learned that Abe harbored a dream to open a barber shop in Ithaca, away from his Lansing in-laws. The two men laughed together, and Abe invited Joe to the couple's blanket to taste some American potato salad. This was perfect! Helen looked directly at Joe and offered him a plate. From the corner of his eye Joe saw Leo headed in their direction, so far oblivious of Joe's whereabouts. He lowered his head toward the plate, in the guise of eating carefully so as not to spill, but in reality hoping to escape Leo's notice. He wasn't yet ready to share his new acquaintances, or least of all, explain them.

The next time they passed one another, she lifted her eyes to him in casual greeting as she strolled into the salt house to begin her day. He alternated between openly observing the athletic prowess of her work when she exited the salt house with a bag on her small back and feigning indifference; consciously avoiding the notice of the Syrian men was crucial. A few weeks later he made his move. She stooped to drop her bag by the train landing one day and he bent over to retrieve a scoop of salt as if pretending she had spilled some. She smirked and grunted, a signal he interpreted as silently acknowledging something between them.

"Can you get away to the lakeshore after supper?" he said in a bare whisper.

"I don't know."

"Try. Meet me at the trestle cover on the tracks, other side, out of sight. We'll walk."

He smoked through four cigarettes before he saw her. She came! But she sauntered right past him, along the track toward the park entrance. It made some sense for her to go that way, away from the men congregated on the bridge, forbidden to her. Joe didn't think anyone could notice but just in case, he smoked another one, then tossed it into the creek and followed south along the track. At the water's edge she was sitting just behind a clump of trees, trying to stay out of sight. Joe crouched two feet away, pretending to study some fish, then looked around for stones to throw. She finally spoke.

"My brother and our people warned me to stay away from you. I told them, 'Never mind about that. I hate him!'"

Laughter exploded from the deepest parts of his body, throat trying but failing to squeeze it down.

"And do you?" His eyes crinkled with the joke, edges of his lips spreading towards his dimples.

Helen looked over at him with the first real grin he'd yet seen on her face, then threw back her head and laughed for a full minute, Joe joining her halfway into it. Had he felt secure in their privacy he would have impulsively grabbed her hand and pulled her along the beachfront to the pier where they could breathe in the water's smells and brush shoulders, while leaning over to watch the waves lap against the dock pilings.

It turned out they got some help with the complicity of Abe and Alice Mahool; the young couple had themselves experienced the bigotry bound up with mixed marriage. Marrying a Syrian boy was not what Alice's parents, an upright family firmly established in the town of Lansing, had in mind for their daughter. Without a blessing, the two had defied her family and married secretly in Ithaca. A year later, Alice gave birth to a baby girl and they celebrated alone, without family.

They understood the pull between Joe and Helen, who managed to keep their bond secret for almost a year. The Mahools offered them unique chances to talk together on Sunday trips to Ithaca to visit friends of Abe, Helen in tow, and Joe not far behind in another train car. One time, they all disembarked in Renwick Park. The bandshell swelled with music and, as the crowds swayed to the band, Joe and Helen took advantage of various intersecting paths, leading away from the others, to anonymously stroll hand in hand. Another week, the foursome visited a group of Syrians for an afternoon feast in the home of Abe and Anna Abbott on West Buffalo Street. Abe Abbott, then the proud owner of a shoe store, was mentoring Abe Mahool in his goal to open a barbershop. Joe liked these Syrians, successful and hardworking yet humble and generous, so unlike the shrewd, hustling Syrians he had encountered in Santo Domingo.

The best opportunities of all were delivered through the haircuts Abe offered at his home, the home where Helen also lived. Joe had a lot of haircuts in the year 1911, always appearing neat and trim, and if anyone noticed the irony, nothing was mentioned. Alice was a true friend and mentor to Helen and helped Helen improve her English. That Christmas the three of them joined the community singing at the storefront and Joe arrived from a discreet distance. He casually pushed his way to stand beside Helen, never looking down at her while he sang, but feeling her body pressed ever so lightly against his side. His blood quickened and he decided in that moment that he'd marry her before the next Christmas.

CHAPTER 12

Forbidden

Myers Park - June 1912

JOE

The winter of 1912 was harsh. Were he not in love, Joe could not have put aside the misery when, all too often, he tunneled his way through the lake winds that sliced corridors between the well buildings and chafed his lips. It was impossible to enjoy a smoke in the freezing air, not that the suffering would stop his trying. Maybe the cold stung worse up on the unprotected hill of Tubbha, but Joe felt hemmed in and isolated down on the flats, only yards away from his Helen. It mattered little to Joe that he spent no time with his brother.

Leo kept company with the younger men, with cards and talk of the old country. And he had been surprised and overjoyed to reconnect with Najeeb and Abraham Simon, boys he had known in school back in Ladehkiya. Joe, realizing that Leo would be affected by any change to their lives and habitation, decided, at last, to confide in his little brother. "Manas, I am going to get married."

The room was silent at first; Joe wondered if he had been heard.

"You think I don't know what you've been up to, brother? You'll never get away with it. They won't let you. Those guys are proud and stupid. The Simon boys already warned me."

"Hah! Think I don't know they'll try to stop us? Just watch!"

"Why suffer the indignity? I don't understand you. All for an *odar*?"

"Manas, have you noticed an Armenian beauty within a day's train ride? I haven't met an Armenian girl since the boat left the Ladehkiya dock. I'm living in the world outside it! Look around you, brother. This is Amirka! Where the old ways melt away and new ones are made." The words burst forth out of an instinct of defense, but the moment they passed his lips, he knew they were true for him. The question Leo had just posed may actually have lingered in some part of his mind before now, but its banishment was instantly complete and final.

He did, however, make it a point to be as nonchalant as possible around Helen for the remainder of the cold months; he hoped she wasn't confused by it. He wanted to throw the Syrians off their guard. As soon as the snows seemed gone for good in mid-April, the community excitedly planned an Easter event. It would begin on the point overlooking the lake at the top of the hill where a priest from Glenn Falls was to visit and give mass. Afterward, the salt block community and local farmers would picnic at the park and hide eggs, American style, for the children. The Ukraine and Hungarian workers' wives painted beautiful designs on eggs that spilled from straw baskets laced through their arms as they paraded to the park and, within moments, decoratively filled the makeshift tables and blankets with color and detail.

Joe hadn't planned at first to attend the Easter Mass. Raised in the Presbyterian tradition by American missionaries he held no interest in the services conducted by visiting priests. But he knew Helen to be a devout Orthodox girl from Melkia, where the villagers suffered for their religion and regularly fended off attacks and thefts from neighboring Muslim villages. He made a gallant effort this Easter. After the mass, Joe scanned the festive scene at the park, searching for the priest. He spotted him by a food table and strolled casually over.

"Father, thank you for your gift to us today. How often do you come to Myers?"

"Thank you, son. I come a few times each year, not always on a holiday."

"When do you imagine might be your next visit?"

"Perhaps in July, or maybe August. Do you have a reason for inquiring?"

Joe shared his desire to marry, then added, "As soon as possible."

"And I presume both you and the bride are Orthodox?"

He recognized the problem immediately. Joe hesitated, then vaguely murmured something in the negative, that was not explicit about his Protestantism or committal about his faith. He thanked the priest again and hurried away. He would not pursue the matter further but knew he must work out a way. Nor should he waste another day; he had to settle the matter with Helen.

By the time the sun dropped behind the hill that rose from the western shore, Joe had still not had a chance to speak privately—or even in code—to Helen. He offered to help Alice carry baskets full of empty plates up the hill. She smiled at him with understanding and gladly acquiesced, hoisting her toddler on her hip. Leo glanced over as Joe set off behind the women and smirked. Joe frankly didn't care, nor did he care what the Syrian men would think or say. He felt ready for the confrontation.

With the baskets deposited in the tiny kitchen on Tubbha Hill, Joe took Helen by the arm and stepped out the side door, gently pulling her after him. She glanced around nervously but the house did not butt against another; it was the last house on the short lane that turned off the main street and faced only trees. He squeezed her hand and she relaxed. He sat her down on a bench outside the door and stood in front of her.

"Helen, shall we marry?" Just like that he blurted it out! He knew no other way to say it.

She gasped and closed her lips, for only a minute but it felt interminable. She is just surprised, Joe told himself, waiting. In truth, he had not much considered her reaction, had simply not doubted her response. Now he wondered if he should have done this differently.

"Are you that fearless?" It was her turn to surprise him.

"Of course."

"Then let's." A simple answer to a simple question. He looked at her again, moved by her no-nonsense character and, in that single moment, secure in the knowledge that she would be with him for the rest of his days; certain too, that he would never regret it. She had a question though.

"Will we marry in secret like Abe and Alice?"

"Nah. Tell your brother. Tell them all. I'll handle them. Better yet, I'll tell your brother."

"No, let me. He does not provide for me and has no hold over me. I'll tell Moses."

They came for him early the next morning, before shifts. They pounded on his door. He swung it open and with a stone-cold face asked, "Okay, who's first?"

Moses stepped forward, fists raised to his chest. Joe stepped down off the door ledge and reached right over those fists, landing the jaw with the first swing. Moses was short and stocky, but had no heart for fighting. He made some more gestures while hopping back and forth but Joe decided to spare him embarrassment.

"Want to continue this after shifts?" Joe's stance was still ready, and he didn't look finished.

Relief and murmur among the group of men was palpable. Moses nodded, growling, "I'm not done." The bravado he attempted to muster into three words pathetically trailed off into a raspy croak by the final word.

After work, the group assembled at the water behind the salt block, presumably away from the eyes of women or the men clustered on the bridge. Yet somehow, word spread like liquid and a crowd quickly formed. Joe wanted only to get it done and over.

"*I'll put all you guys in one shirt!*" His English was intended to show off, for the benefit of the watching crew.

He fought each one of them, six in all, before a truce was struck. Brother Leo appeared and, from off to the side, cheered him with whoops and grunts. Joe took some hard hits, too, but he was two or three inches taller than the men of Melkia and could fend off most of their blows with blocks or by pinning them under his arms. Grudgingly, the men dispersed, and the matter was over. They would not bless the marriage—that was a bridge too far. But it was clear there was nothing they could do about it.

The next challenge was the business of a priest. Helen was adamant they find a priest to marry them. So on Sunday, Joe took the train to Ithaca and visited the Greek Church. That priest, too, refused to marry them. Joe was Protestant; as far as priests were concerned, he may as well have been a heretic. It occurred to him then, with no little amount of appreciation, how tolerant his own people at home were: one third of the population of Kessab were Protestant, one third Catholics, and one third Apostelic, and all lived together harmoniously. Yet these Syrians were ruthlessly prejudiced. Joe wondered if the Syrian Christians were so accustomed to persecution as a minority that they carried their grievances into the new countries with the same bigotry they suffered at home. Shaking his head at the irony, he realized he must break the news honestly to Helen.

He learned later that she sobbed all night. Not to be married by a priest was inconceivable. She said she had thought of her father, Moses Sardo, and contemplated what he would say or do to her, when she later described the result of her thinking to Joe.

"The simple truth is, my father is not here. And my brother may as well not be either, all the good he does for me." The epiphany was liberating for her, she exclaimed with relief.

Alone until now, she was embarking on a new life and wasn't going to miss the train to that life over the matter of who would seal her commitment to God and her husband. Joe laughed and allowed himself a moment to think of his own father, whose potential reaction he couldn't at all imagine. But, he sighed, there was little point to such musing. In the end Alice invited her pastor, Reverend Evans of Lansing Presbyterian, to meet the couple and it was arranged.

The following Saturday, Helen and Alice went to the Abbotts' home in Ithaca. It was a bright weekend in May and the very first time Helen had missed a work shift. Joe learned from Abe that Helen bought shoes with her savings from the store and Anna fitted Helen for a wedding dress. On Sunday, on recommendation from Alice, Joe and Helen rode the Black Diamond train north to Emerson Park in Auburn. The gazebo reminded them of Renwick Park, though the extensively manicured grounds were less familiar. They gratefully felt incognito and at peace as they sat by the lakeshore and talked things through.

The marriage could take place at their own park in Myers. That way, the couple decided, whomever wished to, could attend. Invitations were purposely avoided; nobody need take a position to decline, snub, or accept an invitation. The people of Melkia could stroll through the park and pass by out of curiosity, even pretend not to notice; likewise, they could choose to honor the couple in celebration of Joe and Helen's love for one another. The Reverend Evans officiating, Helen told Joe, her brother would hold against her until he grew tired of his grudge. Her own grudge against Moses was at this point fading; she was too much in love to bother with his disdain for her happiness. Joe had yet to learn how capable she was of holding onto grudges. But on July 7th, 1912, he happily discovered just how gracious were some of the workers, including Syrians such as his pal John Solomon, who witnessed for him. The entire Simon family was preparing to leave for work at a mill factory in Fulton, but delayed the move by several days to attend the ceremony first.

Brother and witness, Leo and John, accompanied Joe to the park and as they bantered about the easy simplicity of the event, Joe was reminded how different this day felt than what he personally knew of a wedding celebration. In Kessab, he had witnessed the festivities of many weddings, weeklong affairs with traditional rituals that survived centuries, including the dressing of the groom by his family and friends. He was about to joke to Leo about this when he choked a little, remembering the scene that would have come next: the bride would ride to the church in the groom's town on a white horse decorated by her family, accompanied by family and friends, with the best man leading the horse. Joe tried to imagine Helen on a white horse but then shook himself with a stark realization: were they in Syria they would not be marrying one another. It is, in fact, unlikely they would have met. God bless, Amirka, he thought, and quickened his pace.

His bride arrived, arms interlaced with Alice, Abe trailing behind and carrying two-year-old Dorthea. A handful of friends had gathered along with the Simons, including Leo Abraham, Tony and Jenny Isaac, and Joe's foreman, McGuire. Joe wished he had sent word to his cousins Asadour and Boghos in Rochester, a sudden craving washing over him for family to witness his happy day. Perhaps it was the reminiscing of Kessab and the large tribe he had been part of and grown so used to that sparked this need. Then he thought that he would not want to burden them with the obligation, imagining the cost for the two train fares to Auburn and on to Myers or even boat transport from the Erie Canal. Joe stood under the sun in new light gray slacks and the white shirt Abe had loaned him. He wished he had taken more care with his wardrobe as he turned his attention to Helen in the white shimmery short sleeve dress made by Anna Abbott.

It was a simple summer affair. Helen's dress was mid-calf length with lace on the sleeves, bodice, and waist. Her shoes and stockings were also white. Her tanned face glowed. Her auburn hair was swept and pinned at the back of her neck; a chain of flowers was attached to a lace veil that lightly brushed her shoulders. When their eyes met his blood quickened, rushing from his toes to groin and belly, causing his heart to speed up. He longed then and there to pick her up and carry her away to the bungalow by the tracks and prayed for a swift ceremony.

As hard as he tried to focus on faces and words, he could not stop his mind from racing to moments ahead. The Manas brothers had conveniently departed after the holiday festivities on the fourth: they, too, moved on to jobs in the new Detroit auto industry. Only Leo remained in the house, now banished to the ground floor living area to sleep so that Joe and Helen could privately share the loft area. But Joe knew that the house would not be suitable for long and living with Leo might be burdensome for Helen. He hoped for the best in the immediate future, under these circumstances, but decided to keep his eyes and ears open for new and better opportunities. After all, the spitfire girl from Melkia was now his wife.

CHAPTER 13

FORD CALLING
Tubbha - January 1913

HELEN

I straighten my back to stand upright and rub my belly without thinking. All seems to be well, though I wonder, would I know the difference? This is my last day hauling and it couldn't come soon enough. Tomorrow I move inside the salt house to bag with the other women, less salary but I don't care. I won't be slipping and sliding over ice, loaded down with salt to break my balance.

The best thing is, we will move to the hill next week! Yussef and me, we will not be bringing our baby into a world of gambling and swearing men crammed into housing on the flats with all their men habits and noise. Abe and Alice have moved to Ithaca to follow Abe's heart—his barbershop—and we will occupy the house they are leaving on Tubbha hill. The little house

155

is next to the Abrahams, Leo and Zahea, and their growing family. Civilization on Tubbha! And Yussef to myself most nights. The thought of it warms me as I turn back to the bagging room for what will be one of my last loads. Daydreaming is the salve against the biting air that blows at me from the lake, trying hard to knock me over. But I feel a warmth creep up my body, thinking through the memory of these past months.

He showed up like a stallion. It immediately seemed that he towered over the men of Syria, though he wasn't really all that high off the ground. Perhaps it was his attitude that made him appear tall. Proud. At first I thought he was full of himself. But the more Moses and the Melki boys griped about the man, the more closely I watched him, that is, when he could not notice my stares. Sometimes I caught him watching me back just as I turned away, but I was not about to reward him with my eyes. Not at first.

I suppose he really had no choice but to play the cock and assume confidence and indifference in order to maintain authority over the workers. They sneer when they call him Bete Armine. So what if he is Armine, as long as he is Orthodox! That was my thought at the beginning. Now I am glad I didn't know that he isn't Orthodox: I might not have what I feel now, or the blessing that stirs inside of me. He speaks better than any of us; he has education! When he grins his face breaks into dimple-rich handsomeness and takes my breath away. I notice that he teases a lot, joking with the men as if he thinks they are laughing along with him and not knowing how they fume with resentment inside. Or, maybe he does know and just doesn't care. Nothing can change the fact that he is boss. Or that I am helplessly over a waterfall with love for him.

"Bete! Bete! Bete Armine! Yallah!"

I am jolted out of my reverie and realize, in slow motion, that the voice yelling is real, is present. They are calling to my husband! I drop the bag I had begun to lift from the ground and rush back out of the building. George Moses is racing toward the boilers, but he needn't bother continuing since I see Yussef already sliding over salt-strewn ice, practically skating in the direction of George's voice. The panic on his face—I've never before seen fear on it—chills me to the bone. It makes me helpless, freezing me where I stand. But only for a minute, because more voices are now adding to the chorus, pulling at our attention. George suddenly stops, doubles over to grab a lungful of air, gasping for the breath he needs to blurt out three words.

"It's your brother!"

Yussef sees me then and his face changes, twisting, alternating in real time between relief and renewed panic for whatever is wrong with Leo. I see in that moment his first thought was of me, and I know for certain I will not lift another bag of salt. Instead, I follow him, carefully picking my way over the ice instead of matching his speed, to the landing by the tracks. Men are clustered around something or someone, and my husband's name is still being called. The bodies part for him. The faces ashen. I can almost feel my Yussef's stomach lurch as he intentionally slows his approach with the dread that must be suffocating him.

The stretcher is a makeshift slab of wood; the body writhing on it is that of Leo. I can only see Yussef from behind now but the way his shoulders repeatedly tense up and then slump, I think he is veering between fear and anger. I witnessed that once before, confronting the men of my village. He knows his anger could threaten to worsen any crisis, so he is swallowing it away. Besides, he must assess the target of his emotion, perhaps the sloppy conditions of the mine and casual attitude the managers hold around safety. Or could it possibly be a reckless action by his impulsive younger brother? I am almost by his side when he clamps his mouth tightly shut and glances over at a doctor pouring alcohol over a saw. My husband's knees give way then, and he would have sank to the ground but for the Solomon brothers who block his fall, each grabbing an armpit to steady him.

He fills his lungs then and screams at them to stop.

"*Take to hospital! Hospital! Now.*" The stress suddenly reducing his English to an incoherent stutter, as bad as mine.

"Are you the brother?" asks the company doctor. Yussef nods, silent now. The man is gentle but firm. "It may be too late, though we sent for a buggy. Gangrene will set in fast."

The next twenty minutes are the longest I can remember. A pattern forms, alternating between Yussef taking charge and losing his self-control. One moment he is clamping a hand on one of Leo's arms, as much to let him know he is there as to physically restrain movement that might cause further harm. Another moment he breaks away from the cluster of men and paces, watching desperately for the buggy to arrive. Four more men are stationed at various limbs, holding Leo still; restraining a soul like this is a responsibility I hope never to be burdened with. Aside from the whiskey poured down his throat and the rag clamped between his teeth, poor Leo is not anesthetized. The salt slide that caught his leg has claimed it. It is unbearable to witness. And it is too late.

My husband's hair turns snow white. In less than one month of the accident, the transformation is complete. I thought it a curse, some kind of hex put upon him. Who can imagine a man of less than twenty-five years with hair as white as cotton? Leo tells me he is not entirely surprised because of their mother's side of the family.

"The Injejikians are known for their men turning gray early in life, in their twenties," he said. "Add that to the stress Hovsep carries around and, voila white hair!"

I bite my tongue at his cavalier comment. Perhaps it was an innocent detail that popped into his head, but it gave the appearance of unconcern for Yussef, as if Leo had nothing to do with it, as if the problem were not triggered by Leo's own crisis. Actually, this is one of the more harmless things to escape this brother's mouth. I pray for him nightly, asking God to ease the pain that is etched throughout his face. Life has dealt him an unfair blow. And to me and Yussef, too. I cannot blame Leo that he is bitter and enraged at his fate. But he has found in me an easy target. And my bridal home happiness is now interrupted, rather cruelly so.

"Helen! Fetch me water! Fetch me the pan!" or "Woman, I'm hungry!" Leo shouts, sending me running for his every need as disrespectfully as to a servant. When he isn't sulking he is demanding the attention of my husband. I can understand his boredom and helplessness, having only a game of cards to look forward to when Yussef comes home from work or from collecting rents at the boarding house. But I am finding myself increasingly lonely at night in bed until Leo will release my husband to sleep. I do not mind that caring for Leo required me to stop work earlier than planned. I try to slip away from the house to visit with Zahea, to steal moments of pleasant company.

"Haloun, you look frazzled and tired. How is Leo?"

"Oh, Zaha, I try to be charitable in my heart to Leo, for Yussef's sake; after all his life has turned with a finger snap. But he ignores the sacrifices we all make for him, and his temper is insufferable."

"Patience, little Haloun," she tells me. "Remember this, too, shall pass." Zahea's calming presence next door again comforts me, not the least because my time is drawing near and she will be on hand to midwife. Midwife Flora—that's what the Amirkans call her—will be the only thing between me and God at that hour. If my child is a girl, I decide, I will name her for this angel, Zahea. I thank her with a sigh and resolve to compose myself as I exit her kitchen door.

I return to a snarl and complaint about something that Leo wanted and went without during my absence. It is not my nature to hold back, but I know if I complain too much to Yussef, his helplessness to the situation will turn on me. He feels responsible for his brother and that it is something beyond me.

My husband has been talking with the company on Leo's behalf, but I doubt that will amount to anything more than throwing steam onto deaf ears. There is some question about how the rail car ran over Leo's leg. I am not clear if the company told him the incident is 'worker error.' This is a new phrase that I am only now hearing in whispers among workers. As far as I am concerned, the company must pay. Everyone says so, not just Yussef and Leo.

"Manas needs a new leg—what is the word? Prosthetic. Something like that," he tells me, pronouncing the word "*prostetik*." "But first he must heal, have the leg fitted, and then…"

The part he leaves unsaid is that Leo may only then be out of our daily home life, but it feels so far away. With every passing day, I am beginning to despair. Most nights, when Yussef remains near the sofa where Leo is sprawled to keep him company and play cards, I lay alone in our bed in my own confusion: both grateful for the break from Leo's demands and disappointed with my daily life. In the old country, we girls were never to go to the well alone, lest we be kidnapped by Muslims. Even when I went with my father, he would hoist me up into a tree when we heard riders come near. During one of these lonely nights in our bed I allow myself to imagine what life could be if I had been stolen by a Muslim rider. A slave to a Muslim household. Would it be like this? Running endlessly to satisfy the whims of one man while growing babies inside? I pushed the thought from my mind, knowing that if I feel sorry for myself, I will deserve an unhappy life. Besides, my husband is the model of a man who does not despair or crumble at a losing hand of cards. I wish to be more like him.

There is much talk among the men who come up the hill to visit with us. Evidently Abraham Simon also had an accident that, before now, we did not know about; I think it was hushed up. He lost his finger and is now moved to a place called Fulton near Syracuse with most of his brothers and parents. My friend Louise is gone with them, her presence missing from the salt house. The oldest brother, Ameen, is planning to leave for a place called Detroit, and when he comes with Najeeb to pay a visit, I overhear Leo speak with him about it. Leo is thinking that with a new leg, Detroit will be the answer for him. It seems Youseef and Manas have another brother there they call Khatchig; I don't know the Arabic name for that, nor the American one. Only Zahea knows how I pray for the day Leo Peter departs for Detroit. And maybe my husband suspects.

May 1913

And come it did, the day I longed for! By spring Leo is gone, gone with his money too! Thank the Lord in Heaven, his terror over me was quickly finished when he got his money and hightailed it out of here. He left in March on the train with Ameen. If his stay was any longer I think I would have exploded from pride and frustration, may even have risked my husband's love, a frightening thought. Our life together is too fresh to be so badly tested. But damn the man! Did he share any bit of the settlement with us after Yussef paid his doctor fee, fought for him with the company, and we fed and housed him for months? Certainly not. At least he is gone. But I will put my foot down if ever again he enters our lives. The future is reserved for my children, and I will not live under the same roof with that miserable brother, no matter what the sacrifice.

There is even more joy upon us. The forsythia still blooms and now the lilacs on Tubbha are in their full purple glory deep into May. My life gratefully revolves around the child almost here, rather than the surly brother that was so long on our sofa, swallowing the air from our home. I can feel Yussef lightening too, though not as much as I. He is carrying some pressure about the company and unsettled business around Leo. I have begged him not to play cards after work or on Sundays, and he comes home to me for supper each night. But I am taken aback when he arrives early on a Friday afternoon, just as I am cooking shadeyah (pilaf) and lubi, my green bean stew with tomatoes, and stuffing the 'cusa' squash with ground meat and onions.

"Well, we are going too!" Stiffening, I pray his words do not mean what I fear.

"Going where?"

"Detroit." One word only. He is not looking at me. Is he afraid of my reaction? I wait.

"I told McGuire I will sue if tey don't finish with Manas' doctor bills and pay. He took me to the big boss; tey said tey'd fire me if I sue. I told tem: 'Never mind. I quit!'"

He switched in and out of English while telling me. And I knew that was that. My proud, impulsive husband would not grovel.

"Yussef, I beg you to promise me one thing. I must have this baby first, in Tubbha. Please do not plan for us to travel until after."

"There are doctors in Detroit. And Ford is paying five dollars a day..." he begins but then thinks again and changes to "Never mind. It's good. I will use the time to sell the boarding house and settle business. Then we go."

My time begins on the 21st day of May, but the pushing lasts until the next morning. At last, the woman Alice brought to help Zahea lays the boy in my arms. The moment Henna latches to my breast I regret having agreed to the move. I do not know the word in English for mourning but this is what I am feeling. I am with a newborn child, nursing Henna endlessly, not strong enough to carry my own bag, and my Youssef wants to drag us to a new world. I know he needs the work and expects a better income in Detroit.

A city, though! He told me how he hated the big city we first came to in this land. I just hope we do not sink into a hole he cannot stomach. I've seen his temper only twice, but I can imagine the rage simmering down below and easily erupting in a place and time of unjust things. He has hinted at such things in the old country. I am also filled with unease, leaving behind all that I know of Amirka, and Moses, Alice, Zahea, Anna Abbott, the women I trust.

Who will I talk with? My thoughts bounce between dread and sadness and then, at last, resolve. In my heart I already know I will trust my man and put on a brave face. We are married less than one year and if I think about the beginnings… My insides warm all over again. Yussef tells me, "You're gonna like Khatchig, so different from Manas. A kind man."

And I tell him, "The Melkia men now call you Abu Henna behind your back." I say it to make him proud. It means Father of John. He looks at little Henna then and smiles.

"Shall we make some more like this?" The dimples appear when he grins.

CHAPTER 14

SALT AND SOIL

Detroit – 1913

HELEN

When we board the train, Yussef moves us from car to car, looking for the most space to stretch out in. Finally, we sit—I actually sink—and slide the cases under our feet to use as footrests for the long ride. I cling to the little one in my arms, peeking at his face constantly to make sure I haven't squeezed him too hard. Only two weeks old, my little Henna, and off to a new life. For now and until we are settled in a home, I will defer to my husband for everything, even when we will eat. I unwrap the stuffed cusa and tabouli I have packed in my basket and offer some to Yussef. Joe. I am practicing his Amirkan name since he thinks it easier when we travel alone like this. I look at him, my Joe.

Excitement is in his face. Adventure is his salvation. I have not seen him show fear, not of my brother and countrymen, nor of the bosses at the salt block. This can be a good thing or maybe a bad thing; there is no denying it. But he will always make things right. Of that I have no doubt, and I swallow away my unease.

Can it be only three years since I boarded a boat in Beyruth and watched the waves push me to a new life on this side of the world? I knew nothing then of what my life could look like, be like. Now, I study this family of mine: a good and decent man who I would follow to the ends of the earth, and this child. I look at my sleeping son, so new to this earth, and think, so handsome he is, like his father. When he wakes, I have to think about how I will feed him privately. I reach over and squeeze the hand closest to me. Joe. Joe Peter.

He says, "*Tey say Ford is paying five dollar a day. Tat* will be double what I made at the salt block. I will find us a house as soon as I begin." I know he is practicing English, but he gives up and switches back to our Syrian words.

"But until then? Where will we be?" I interrupt, I can't help it; my stomach has lurched at a thought that only now appears in my mind. My husband is looking at me, at my heart.

"Don't worry, Haloun. If even for a few days we must stay with Khatchig and Manas while I look around, you will not be under Manas' thumb. I promise."

The city is larger than any I have been, except the big one where the boat landed and, of course, Beyrouth. By September, we are settled on one floor of a three-family house in Highland Park quite swiftly, and near many other young families. In the summer, the Simon family appears in the neighborhood, and so I am reunited with my dear friend, Louise! She coos over little Henna and provides me an opportunity to walk about among the swarming streets full of people like us, and those from other countries, too. Louise's family surprises me with a carriage for Henna—a gift from a church they attend that is not like my church. Like, Yussef, they were connected to missionaries of Protestant faith. I choose not to think about it, the confusion is great and not worth interfering with my few daily pleasures. Nights are not dark and silent as they had been in Tubbha— the lamps and sounds of the street are unsettling. But climbing into my husband's embrace is always a relief. And often a delight.

Yussef had not waited in line at the Ford employment queue. He took one look at the big crowd there and walked over to the Maxwell plant that was showing the same employment sign. He asked the pay rate—also five dollars a day—and signed on. My husband has little patience, but I suppose there is no harm done, so long as the outcome is good.

The whole city is abuzz with automobile talk. And in so many languages! But there are plenty of Arabic speakers everywhere I turn. I can walk out on the streets pushing Henna's pram without fear. And with so many of the Orthodox faith, there is a big church nearby! On Sunday mornings Yussef watches Henna (John) as I attend mass. And often I attend other days at five in the afternoon with my child; Henna is mercifully calm in the big church, and I make sure to nurse him first so he will sleep. After, there is still time to prepare supper before Yussef's shift ends. Just as I am feeling comfortable in our new world, my spirit sings to feel a new life stirring again inside.

But not one half year since we got off the train that brought us from Ithaca, Yussef is at it again!

"Helen! We are moving!"

He found a small farm of ten acres to rent in another place called Port Hune! Just like that! I cannot find words before my face shows them.

"Don't worry! There is a salt plant there. I can work and grow the vegetables. And get out of this God forsaken city all in one win!" I hate it when he uses phrases that relate our lives to a card game.

Port Hune turns out to be a happy dream! We moved when the colors were boasting their brightest reds. Yussef was happy to clear out a large vegetable garden before the snows fly and instantly plan for the spring. He is even now collecting seeds. My stomach has swelled to bursting with little John's new sibling; my Jirgis will arrive with the greening of the garden in spring. A whole community of Syrians live nearby. And the big bonus: a priest! He comes to our house on Sundays to give mass and our countrymen stay for lunch. Sundays are my happy days. The house fills with plates of loobi, stuffed koussas and cabbages, taboulis, pilaf, dolma, and the moonshine my husband has secretly begun to brew in a still hidden down in our cellar. All of this mingles with chatter about the old country and child births among the women. It surpasses even the feeling of home on Tubbha Hill and fills my heart with comfort. This is especially true since my brother has decided to come here also. He followed us to Detroit and met his bride, Mary, there. Last month he learned of the salt wells here at the lake and prefers what he knows of salt production to auto factories. It will be nice to have family of my own nearby.

What I love the most about this home we are creating is when I stand on the porch, or the slopes above the house, and gaze at the water of Lake Hune. It is sometimes blue, sometimes the color of steel, and you cannot see the other shore like at Lake Cayuga at Tubbha. I understand now that I wish always to live on a hill from where I can see the world around me and take into my eyes all that is more important than any of the troubles that may lurk below. Or inside our own home.

It is well into winter when we have a surprise visitor. Thank God, Yussef is home when he walks up the road toward the gardens or I might have frightened him off by my fear of trying out the new language. I see the man out of the window—too tall to be Syrian, but dark-eyed nonetheless—walk with an easy stride that is similar to the Armenian men of my new family.

I don't know if Yussef has seen him, so I go to the porch and call in my small bit of English, in case the man is American, "Josef! Man comink!" My husband sets down the shovel he'd been working with and approaches, while I rush back inside to avoid the cold air. I watch from the window. You can hear every sound from up here on top of the world where words and grunts and birdsong bounce and amplify on the open air currents. Yussef stops suddenly, one hand shading his squinting eyes against the glare as the profile of the man gets closer, blocking the sun, a silhouette in black.

"Asadour?" My heart pounds immediately and I stifle a gasp. The only time I heard Yussef speak of his brother Asadour, it was with great pain. He had lost him, lost touch entirely. He always changes the subject when the other brothers mention this brother, and I think maybe he harbors some guilt, having left Asadour on an island in the southern seas.

But then he says, "Cousin? Cousin! Barev, Asadour!" He said it first in Arabic. I realize he is repeating himself in Armenian. I throw on a shawl and return to the porch to witness what I imagine is, must be, important. He had traveled, this cousin, from Rochester, New York by way of Canada and over the Michigan border to us. Not to Detroit, not to the others. I wonder why.

"Oh, Hovsep, I'm so glad to find you. It was difficult. I sent cable to Detroit, Leo sent this address. I didn't want to lose more time... came straight—"

"Asadour, come inside; warm up with tea and Arak. Then you speak. Come." Yussef interrupts and the two embrace while I scramble back inside to the kitchen to put up the kettle. I put together a plate of tabouli, dolma, and olives. It has finally dawned on me the poor man, this cousin, is probably starving.

After introductions, Asadour tries to speak again, but we insist he eat first. Finally, "Hovsep, I come with sad news. I'm so sorry…" His face holds no longer and he is sobbing. I see, no, feel my husband stiffen and prepare himself for what is coming; we remain silent. I cannot follow much Armenian, but the message is quite clear and I can ask for details later.

"Your father is dead," he blurts it as if spitting the words will make it less true or painful.

Yussef's face crumples, shoulders tremble then sink to a stillness like the blanket of snow surrounding the house. The moment stretches long. The tears are slow to come and when they do, he doesn't bother to wipe them away.

Still silent, he seems to know there is more, asks, "And Mary and Marta?" I know Mary to be a sister, red-haired and beautiful, and whatever Asadour is trying to say, trying to answer the question, is too hard. Finally, "Mary… Mary was taken." He croaks it out, then lowers his head, as if in shame.

"Taken? What do you mean?!" With a snap, Yussef is on his feet, crouching into the kind of stance that I know will launch the pacing back and forth across our main room. As Yussef paces, Asadour looks up from the table. His eyes look haunted.

"She was taken by Turks, Hovsep. My father telegraphed me to find you." The man, younger than my husband, looks as much like him as do the brothers. He hesitates, gulps, continues, "They came to the shop as Mary delivered the evening tea. Your father, he tried to save her, Hovsep. They stabbed him. Hagop, too! They killed them both. Uncle Bedros, Uncle Hagop..." he trails off, sobbing.

Yussef is still as stone at first, then swallows, squeezes his eyes shut. I, too, am frozen in dread and fear for him, even knowing only the words for 'father...hayrig, and... stab.' Eyes still closed, he asks in a strangled voice, "Nishan. Was Nishan there?" but then bolts upright; I see a new thought suddenly blast through him. "Marta! What of Marta?"

"Nishan was away from the shop but when he returned, the other shopkeepers were waiting for him. They told him. They attended to... the bodies, so that he could collect Marta from school. She is with him and his family and helping with the children."

Even I feel the relief of this last statement. Marta is safe, but she has been taken out of school. Yussef boasted to me about Marta's schooling. What a lucky girl she had been to go to school, even for a time. To me, such a thing, unimaginable. And she is already fourteen. My wandering thoughts are not helpful in this moment. Asadour is speaking again.

"My father says we must try to save Mary. The missionaries may help... but no matter, we need some connections to find where she is taken to. Louisa—do you remember my fiancée, Louisa Guzelian?—she teaches with the missionaries in Kessab, but does not know those of… Do you and your brothers still know missionaries in Ladehkiya? She writes that you must try to make connection. Hayrig can try to assemble manpower in Kessab, but knowledge of Ladehkiya…"

Yussef is pacing again, thinking, swearing in my language, repeating. Finally he comes to a thought that halts him, the one he had been mentally searching for.

"I DO know someone, Asadour. He worked with the missionaries in Ladehkiya… He has family in the area… Maybe he can help us locate her…" He sits down in front of his cousin, excitedly. "Asadour, can you come with me to Detroit?"

"Oh, Hovsep, I can stay only this night, then I must return. I am missing exams already. But perhaps…" he thinks for a minute, then, "the train from Detroit may be even faster. Yes, I'll go with you."

They leave in the morning to find Eassa Simon, Louise's father. For two long days I wait. Yussef returns and sinks into bed, exhausted. A plan has been hatched, but my husband will no longer sleep well. His worry and grief are saved up all day long to haunt him in the dark. I pray for his soul. And for his father's. And for Mary and Marta, my sisters-in-law in the old country, dear ones I may never know.

CHAPTER 15

TROUBLE

Kessab, Latakia - January 1914

ALICE KARAMARDIAN

There erupts a commotion in the house and Mayrig is clearly frightened as she frantically gathers up garments for my four-year-old brother, Vahan. She calls to me and my sister to stuff some nightclothes and a set of day clothes into the satchel she tossed into the bedroom. I am not yet ten years and Vartouhi barely eight. When my father hurriedly packs us into our cart for the day trip to Uncle Bedros' home in Ladekiyah, I assume there is danger from Turks, though I also overheard whispers about Kurdish men roaming about the mountains, planning to attack the village. Everyone is taking the rumors very seriously. We must, ever since the big attack on Kessab when I was four.

We also went to Uncle Bedros' home then, but I do not recall much of that visit, except for the nervousness. It was the first time I could see my father and mother afraid, and this frightened me, so I was grateful to sleep with my older cousins and not alone. My sister, Vartouhi, was only two then and understood nothing; Mayrig kept her close. I learned later that most of the other people from town rushed to Ladekiyah as well, but some of the young men and boys stayed back to keep the Turkish attackers from following us. Half of them died for it, were killed by the Turk monsters. When we returned that time—I think we were away for several weeks—and Hayrig guided the creaky cart slowly up the steep road to home, I saw the old women wandering our streets of Kessab, wailing and crying for the lost men and boys. Then Mayrig cried, too, when we reached our home. Where our house had stood, there was only a big pile of stones and boulders. It felt like a very long time until the house could be built again, and for most of the year, until after I turned five, we stayed at the home of Uncle Giragos in Kaladouran. When it became summer and warm at night we (just my father, mother, Vartouhi, and me) often slept in a tent in the gardens or on the sand at the beach below. I especially remember the stars flashing in the black sky, while invisible waves slapped inside the inky world outside our tent. And when the sun rose in the sky, there were my boy cousins for me to follow around. They were big boys, teenagers, and did not pay me any mind. But I heard them mutter about life in Kessab and talk of somewhere called Amirka.

This time we have packed up again, but I am a big girl and, even though I am prickly with fear, I cannot help but feel excited to go to the home of my sophisticated city cousins, Marta and Mary. I run into the house with the circular kitchen and stone tonir (oven) that takes up a whole wall and look for the girls I have played with each summer when they join the family at Kaladouran for the warm months. Marta is already thirteen, almost a lady, and she allows me to follow her everywhere! Marta is dark-haired just like her mother, it is said, though she has the same sort of eye like her father and brother that seems to float towards her nose. The two of us trail Mary everywhere; she is our queen!

Mary is stunningly beautiful with glowing deep red hair, a color that Syrian women try to create on their hair with henna, but cannot succeed. She is seventeen and a big attraction in the family; it is difficult for strangers to avert their eyes from her. Mary does all the cleaning in the house, and Marta helps her with the cooking when she is not in school. I know Mary walks Marta to and from school and that this is their special time together when they are not bothered by chores and duties. Mary must be so lonely—she had to stop going to school after third year to manage the house. School is very important to all the girls in our family, and I wonder why I have never heard Mary complain of her loss. But she will not allow Marta to lose her education. She is like a mother, and I know a secret between the two girls: Mary has promised Marta she will not marry and abandon her.

I hang around the house as much as possible to watch and be near Mary. Marta and I are like her subjects and we will do anything she tells us to. I enjoy spending an afternoon twisting the wet olive oil bread dough, shaping the strands like knots to form the Pigegh, and letting it bake until the smell brings the men and little Zaha and Mary—cousin Nishan's children—running for a bite. There are five of us working. Another aunt has joined my mother in the big kitchen to help, and Mary seems so grateful to have the older women here. They talk and talk, leaving me and Marta out. We eventually slip away with our small loaves and skip into the garden and the shade of the grape arbor where we can do our own talking, although I know so little that it really is more like me listening to Marta talk; this suits me just fine. It is chilly, just after the January Christmas holiday and, even in my shawl, I shiver. But I hang onto Marta's every word since Mary says so little, and this is the only way I will learn anything. Marta chatters on and on about school. Her school in the city is a mission school like mine, but filled with Arab girls, too, who are some kind of Christian and keep their heads bare, just like us. Marta also has news.

"We haven't heard from my brother Hovsep in four years, but Manas wrote us that Hovsep has married and welcomed a son, born last May..." I do not have a memory of Hovsep; I was barely born when he "disappeared," as the stories say.

"But you will never believe, Elisa!" Marta could not wait to tell me more. "His wife—imagine this, Elisa—he married an Arab girl! A Christian girl, but not Armenian!" My chin dropped appropriately to my neck, mouth dangling to show proper respect for the startling information. But actually, I have never heard of a marriage between an Armenian and an *odar*—anyone else—and could not figure out how to consider it.

When we return to the kitchen the talk there is still abuzz with news of the brothers in Amirka that came in Manas' letter. Manas has even mentioned new names that the brothers use and he spelled them out in Arabic, but I cannot capture the English words.

"*Li – oh ... Jo - sef Pi – tuhr!*" Mary tried to sound them out but my ears will not comprehend.

All this talk of Amirka—the continent to the north, rather than the southern one where most boys who leave Kessab seem to settle—sets my mind to wandering in many directions until it finally lands on a thought: I wonder if girls in Amirka go to school and study before marrying. If not, I would not want to go there. I love school more than anything in the world, except Mayrig, Hayrig. And Vartouhi. And even Vahan. And, of course my teacher, Louisa.

After two weeks, the troubles seem to have faded away and Father says it is safe to go home. Disappointed, I pack my small satchel of things: writing book and a sweater, second shawl, skirt, and sleeping dress. The cart squeaks and squeals and seems to mock my despair at saying goodbye to Mary and Marta. The trip home takes half a day. This time, I prepare myself to confront a pile of boulders when the donkey turns onto our street, hooves pinging against stones as he clamors uphill, but, thank the Lord, our home is intact. We unpack the cart and Father leads the horse to a stable a little down the street that is shared by six families.

It is now February, the holidays are behind us, and I looked forward to returning to school in a few weeks. But before that time comes—we are not home but a few weeks—my Uncle Giragos bursts into our house!

"Bedros is gone! They took Mary!" He is sobbing, gulping, unable to get the words out.

Hayrig tells him to swallow and breathe and, "Start from the beginning!"

"That is all I know! The dogs were waiting when Mary brought supper to the shop. I'll bet they had picked her out for some time and haggled over who would get her. The bastards!"

"Slow down, Giragos. What of Hagop? Nishan? Marta? Do you know anything of them?"

"Only that someone in the quarter ran to the school to tell the missionaries. Perhaps they collected Marta and took her to Nishan's. I know nothing of Hagop. But they stabbed Bedros as he tried to hold onto Mary." Uncle collapses in a heap. Mayrig runs to him with tea.

Through the next days, family bustles in and out of our house. Uncles Hagop and Bedros have both died. I am not sure how, but they must have been together trying to save Mary from her fate. I am still in disbelief, after the long night of shock the day Nishan came to inform us. He closed the shop and carried the bodies home to Kessab in his cart with his wife Louise, Marta, and the children sprawled on top. They all sleep on a floor at Uncle Giragos' in Kaladouran and Uncle Bedros is laid out in mourning in his old home. I beg Marta to stay in our house, but she only looks at me blankly and, with ashen face, stammers that she must stay with Nishan.

My heart breaks for her, she is so alone now. My heart fears for Mary; only God knows what she is enduring at the hands of cruel Turks. And for Uncles

Bedros and Hagop, may God rest and protect their souls. In this week of mourning that includes church each evening and meals each afternoon, ample talk eventually clears things up to me. Mary usually took tea and bread in the afternoon to her father and Uncle Hagop at the shoe shop. A Turkish gendarme who probably admired her beauty decided to help himself. Maybe he watched her for days as she arrived, always at the same time, and chose that moment. Nishan was elsewhere, on an errand, and returned to the shock of carnage. The first thing he did was to collect Marta from school; Mary would have been on her way to do so directly from the shoe shop. He took her home to Lucine and the children, checked on the family and the house, then returned to the shop to face the gruesome reality.

After church service on the sixth night, all the Karamardian men leave Kaladouran and come to our house in the center of town. I am supposed to be asleep with my siblings, but wide awake, I silently slip into a nook in the wall outside the kitchen where the men are seated around the stove, smoking and talking in subdued tones. I settle my bottom onto the tiled floor and lean lightly against the wall to eavesdrop, even though I know I will catch the devil if am caught. But it feels too important to miss.

"What is there to do, Nishan? If you ask questions, you will only put your womenfolk at risk." I recognize my father's voice in the question, but not the voice that responds.

"Of course, he can do no asking! But has he no connections with the missionaries?"

"He did not attend the school in Ladehkiya Besides, even the missionaries are helpless. They can communicate with the local gendarmes, but will receive no help. They need a connection inside the community for any hope to find where she was taken." This is Uncle Giragos' voice. He sounds more assured and reasonable than the day he brought us the news.

"I will send a telegram to my Asadour," he continues. "Perhaps he can reach the sons of Bedros...." Uncle's son is named Asadour, just like my father and another cousin, Mary and Marta's brother who left with Hovsep long ago. There are as many Asadours in our family as there as Khatchigs, and also Marys.

"And that will serve how?" It must be Uncle Stepan, but I am not certain.

"I don't know!" my uncle snaps, his voice rising in frustration. "But don't you think the boys should be informed of their father's death?!"

A silence. I swear I can feel shame emanating from the menfolk. Do they recognize an oversight of not considering my cousins in Amirka? I wonder how the news will reach them. What will it feel like if someone were to tell me my father and mother were gone? Oh, no! I push these thoughts aside with determined force, unwilling to imagine the unimaginable.

The men talk some more, but it fades into an interminable drone in the back of my sleepy mind as I begin to doze on the cold floor. I shake myself and tiptoe back to the children's room where I dream of all my family floating by in my head one by one, including even my unfamiliar cousin in Amirka, Hovsep and his Syrian wife. And Mary in a strange place, scrubbing a floor, and, finally, Marta.

Poor Marta. In one afternoon she has lost her father and sister, everything she has in this world save for Nishan, her nieces and nephews. The other brothers have all left this side of the world forever. She never knew her mother, dead from giving birth to her and buried in Kaladouran. This week we will bury Uncle Bedros next to my aunt on the sloping gorge under a pomegranate tree.

I am luckier in my Kessab bubble for now. Safe with my people. And school. I pray obsessively for Marta. For Mary. For all of us. And then I am fast asleep, all thoughts melted into a vaporous nothing…

CHAPTER 16

STOLEN

Northern Syria - April 1914

MARY KARAMARDIAN

I will not speak of this.

First, there is no one to speak to. Were I to one day escape these wretched, horrid circumstances, who might there be to tell? Father struck down trying to hold onto me, trying to tear me away from disgusting arms that seized me. Marta? Will I ever see her again? Brother Nishan? Are they alive? Even if they are, this, this—whatever you could call my life now—this is inexplicable.

I imagine I will not survive long here anyway. The men will tear me apart at whim. The women hate me and will punish me more. They are the dogs of this world, and yet the world is upside down and inside out. The dogs calling the victims dogs! I think of my mother, whose face I barely recall, but what would calling her name accomplish? She, like anyone, could neither comprehend what is happening to me, nor save me from it.

On Wednesdays I am spared an hour from 'other duties' to fetch the morning water. The well, though not public and owned by my dog master family, is open to some neighbors in the district to use, so I am accustomed to regularly seeing some faces that do not belong inside the compound. Their Muslim rule forbids me to leave my hair free and I am glad of it, since my red locks usually attract unwanted attention. From the time I was snatched from my home and the beloved people who cherished me, attention can only mean pain or humiliation. I exist now as a toy to be played with, discarded, abused. My shiny red hair is a liability. Worse: it is cause for envy and resentment among the women in this Turkish dog household.

Collecting the bucket, I am reminded of the last Wednesday that I approached the well, when I noticed two faces I had never seen before, lurking by the well. My body had naturally tensed, I jerked my eyes away and prepared my radar for danger while I dipped, then hoisted the full bucket to my shoulder and hurried back to the gates. If a man outside the household should catch me, I will be beaten and possibly killed. I am almost, but not quite, ready for that fate. Again, I cannot speak—nor will I think—of the hours of agony my life has endured since that last trip to the well. Today, one week since, I proceed again, armed with bucket and head scarf, ever vigilant against strange faces. I set the bucket down by the rim and, while kneeling, glance up long enough to catch something gleam in the morning light. Instinctively, my eyes cannot help but turn toward the light. Something gold is flashing. Wait! Can it be? A khachkar! Now it is gone. There it is again, catching light from the sun every few seconds.

I'll never know what possessed me to allow my eyes to rise and look directly in the direction of the gold. I can sense there are a few others who glance at the flash but then, seeing nothing further, turn back to their buckets. Against my better judgement, my eyes creep slowly upward to a hand that is holding the object. Yes! It is indeed the Armenian cross. Comprehension eludes me for a moment. I am lost in a trance with peripheral memories threatening to flood into my head, but I suck in my breath, I carefully look again, and yes! I am able to confirm its authenticity! Now... glancing up a bit further to a face and then eyes that are gazing steadily at me! I stare back for several seconds, forgetting for a moment where I am and that I am holding in air. Just as the sensation of danger begins to crawl backward up my spine— still unable to avert my gaze—those eyes across the well soften and the head encasing them now performs an almost imperceptible nod. I exhale as slowly as a certain comprehension invades my brain. He knows I am Armenian; he is not an enemy! He turns and walks away, casually, to avoid attention. And I begin to understand that something is required of me, perhaps something dangerous.

There is no danger that can worsen my situation. Even death will be welcome rather than to remain here for a lifetime. Perhaps I am called upon to do some service for somebody, for my people, before my time is come. I cannot imagine how, but I welcome and rejoice in such an opportunity, and I count the days until the next Wednesday. When the day comes, I collect my bucket and this time, as inconspicuously as I am able, I manage to set it down on the opposite side of the well. As of yet, I see no one about. Perhaps I came too early and will not be able to linger long without arousing suspicion and wrath upon return. I am feeling prickly, waiting for a sound from behind me while cautiously looking about for neighbors or household occupants to appear and possibly thwart my moment with a Christian stranger. Then it comes. Softly, so softly….

"Barev, Miriam" from behind, over my shoulder. Then, "Kefeck." Oh, is the man Armenian or Syrian?

Confused I answer in Arabic, "What do you want?"

"To rescue you. Next week, come ten minutes early." Then… nothing. He is gone.

Was it a trick? I dare not look behind. Oh, my Lord in Heaven, who can want to save me? Father is gone; I saw it with my own eyes. And, in spite of weeks of success at holding up a great barricade against consciousness by numbing my mind, my thoughts are now off and running, memories and concern tumbling over and onward with no control, down the bottomless well of despair.

What happened to poor Marta when I was not there to collect her from school? Is Nishan alive? Who on earth could be risking their lives to pluck me from this hell?

I think at first I will not believe this. I could not survive the disappointment and feel it best to think no more of it. Then I think about the worst case: should I be caught and therefore killed for punishment or sport? Well, then. Death would be welcome. The more I consider the risk, the more I consider it to be nothing. On Wednesday morning, without sleep, I arise early, put on both my skirts and wrap an extra shawl around my waist, though the April air is balmy. I carefully cover my hair, grab the bucket, and hurry down the path to the gate, praying I will attract no attention.

Parking myself in the same spot along the outer edge of the well, I set down the bucket and silently pray for direction from the 'angel voice' before I am noticed.

It is only a moment more when I hear it; in Arabic so quietly, as if from Heaven that I imagine only I can hear.

"Back up slowly. Keep your eyes on the well..."

I follow the direction of the voice with my back and my feet, and just as I mentally take in the first sounds of neighbors approaching the area for the morning water collection, strange arms have gathered me and whisked me out of eyesight, leaving the bucket in the place where I had set it. I am aware of other voices, a few in Turkish but most calling out morning greetings to one another in typical guttural Arabic syllables. I am carefully laid in a cart, told to lie still, and a blanket is wrapped over me. I smell citrus, figs, and pomegranates—crates surrounding me, creating a border between me and the outside world, and I am overcome with a sudden hunger. I fantasize reaching into a crate and helping myself to a sweet fig, but immediately consider the danger ahead. I know I must not move a muscle until instructed otherwise. The questions that grip me will have to wait, and I steel my mind to the sort of numbness that I have practiced for many weeks now, perfected in order to endure the unendurable. But a tiny ember has begun to spark in a cranny at the back of my brain and I cannot resist—ever so gradually—recognizing the sensation. It is hope!

I do not know the village in which I have been held hostage these many weeks. On the day of my abduction,

I had tried to watch the paths the cart traveled, from the center of the Armenian quarter to the compound somewhere outside the city. But as the sun lowered and we were past the old walls of the city, the cart passed through unfamiliar roads that I did not recognize. The day had darkened completely by the time I was dragged out of the cart and presented to two scornful women to bathe me for… what was to come next.

But I can tell this cart is not heading back into Ladehkiya—not to my home—and I despair! I sense that we are traveling south. Or are we traveling east? I am at once unsure and queasy, and now freshly concerned for my safety. I laugh scornfully at myself, remembering how, just hours ago, I had welcomed death. I will myself to numbness once more. After the sun rises high in the sky and I have stopped shivering from the cooler breezes that suggest we are in the mountains, the cart slows to a stop and hands remove my canvas cover and help me to sit up. They are gentle hands, but I dare not look at the face attached to the arms that extend from them. I do, however, take a long, yearning look at the fruit crated beside me and the hands become merciful, passing me some figs, and then a vessel with liquid to take a long drink. I know whomever this is can be no Turk and feel less tentative with each swallow.

"Why am I not being taken home?"

"It is not safe." The voice is the same voice from the well. I lift my eyes to the face.

And my sister, I think to myself, but do not yet dare ask more than necessary.

"Then where do I go?"

"To a town east of here. You will not be recognized there and kept safe. But first we must circle..."

"But..."

"All will be revealed in time. My job is to deliver you, please be patient." And then, as an afterthought, "My name is Abraham." My shoulders relax at this disclosure. He has a Christian name; again, I feel safe.

With a gesture by the man—Abraham—I am summoned to sit up front, and to wrap my head scarf tightly, concealing my hair, to disguise my race. The lowering sun is almost on the horizon when the cart rolls into Mazirah, or called Muzayraa in Arabic, a town I have heard mentioned by Father and various customers in the shoe shop. I immediately regret thinking of my father and instead concentrate on studying the narrow streets, the market, and finally, the gate we pass through to a two-story house. It occurs to me that this place is much closer to Ladehkiya than the distance we have traveled, straight east of my city. It has taken us all day long to travel what should have taken just a few hours in a cart.

Abraham explains as we pull into the courtyard beyond the gate, "We have ridden in many circles, because this would be the first road patrolled that led out of your master's neighborhood. We went south—away from Christian neighborhoods where they will search first—and delayed for a good while, then circled back two times before coming in this direction. Since this is a Christian town, it was likely the first suspected. But since gendarme patrols have not found us on the roads leading east or north to Kessab, they are by now searching the southern routes. God willing."

A man is quickly beside us, helping me down from the cart with a strong arm. He is elderly, yet husky, with a solid body and a kind face that reminds me of my Uncle Garabet.

"Welcome, Maryam!" There are also three women now hurrying down the stone staircase. From the kitchen, I presume, as in so many two-story homes. They touch my face with gentle fingers and also my hair since the scarf has fallen open to my shoulders.

A feeling comes over me that I had imagined I would never feel again. It resembles security, but I dare not succumb to it. Not yet. I know nothing, least of all news of my family. Who are these people and why are they helping me? When they lead me to the kitchen and sit me down, the plate of steaming food in front of me prompts me to weep openly. They call their pilaf *shadiyeh* and the stew covering it has bits of fried lamb among green beans and tomatoes. My stomach roars with joy and it occurs to me I have not eaten meat since I was thrust into the Turkish household. No! I will not think of that. Besides, the man has begun to talk.

"Mary, this is a safe home. This is where you will stay until your travel papers are arranged." My eyes open so wide they seem to be reaching for my brows. I need not have asked because he continues, and the women crowd around, nodding and smiling.

"My name is Boutris. I have a brother in America. My brother knows your brother." The confusion must be all over my face, because he laughs and says, "Let me slow down. Connections have been made with your brothers in Amirka, as well a cousin. You will remain here in our household, under the pretense of a Muslim maid until safe passage is secured. You must continue to cover your red hair as a Muslim would; it is too unique. There are many steps until then. When we receive the word, we must move you to Beyruth. My nephew will accompany you to New York…"

I am thinking, spinning away in my thoughts, the first, oddly, is that this man has my father's name, Bedros. And I wonder, are my brothers in New York? I recall another place in the letter. But Boutris is still talking, so I try to focus.

"… someone will meet you and accompany you to Michigan. It is not clear yet. You will marry…"

Please, I silently pray, say no more! I couldn't take in more, not yet. There was too much said—even more remains unsaid—and I feel my eyes close, causing his voice to trail off. But I swallow for courage to find a voice from somewhere in the back of my throat.

"What of my sister? My family in Ladehkiya?" The panic had risen from my throat to my voice, my face, my stiffening back…

"Dear, Maryam. It is not safe for you to reunite with your brother or sister in Lattakia. Not now. Not for you and not for them. They are alive, that is all I know. You are lucky, too, so you must survive and do justice for the people who will see to your journey. Perhaps, after you settle in the new world, you can send for your sister."

I sleep fitfully that night, but much better in the following nights. Resigning myself to my fate is now a habit that is not so hard to continue. And sleep becomes fearless after the first night here proves to be a night of free, unmolested repose. I make myself a promise when the first light comes—the first light of my freedom. I will survive for the sake of these angels, for the sake of the strangers helping me, rescuing me. And should I escape from the personal danger of my own country, I will lead a truly good life. The man mentioned marriage.

Never mind, it matters not. Whatever is in store will be. If it involves my family, I will trust the outcome. Amirka! Me? But... but what will I have left behind?!

My father, oh my God in Heaven! My father is gone. I saw it in that fateful moment. I saw the knife as he reached for me. And my sister? Perhaps she is safe for now, but how can she thrive without me? Will Nishan see to her education? I pray it be so. My heart heaves with the awareness of my new reality—an awareness I have pushed down to the depths of my stomach in willing myself to survive the past weeks—now crashing upon me, a tsunami, I cannot breathe. It is drowning me. I let myself sob now, and for the next five nights, until I am summoned to gather my belongings of one extra skirt and prepare for a journey, to Beyruth, I presume.

It saddens me to look on the face of Boutris now that the purpose is farewell. Yunnus is the new face to study. I will be at his mercy now for a very long time.

Boutris assures me, "Maryam, you must put your trust in Yunnus, as do I. He is young and will pretend to be your husband in public places; it is the only way you can travel. You will be Mary Simon, using our surname for the journey. Besides, it is your future name."

I decide to ignore the question forming—future name?—and climb into the donkey cart. Crates of supplies have been loaded, which I assumed were a decoy. But had I known we would need all of it, I should have been alarmed and frightened by the significance of how this was going to be a long and hard journey.

And long and hard it is. Rather than take either road west or north, we head straight to the south on no road at all. We drive on a donkey trail right over the mountain! We left at first light but at high noon we only just reach its crest. Much of the time we climb down from the cart and push it, to help the donkey. The poor animal is much too small to pull it on the narrow, steep paths. By dark we reach the bottom of the mountain at Jubayriyah, a village so inconsequential I was surprised Yunnus found lodging in a small inn home. The Muslim family owners were silent but polite, and I was careful to pull my headscarf tightly about my face as they showed us to the room with one small bed. Yunnus motions me to sleep in the bed as he stretches out on the floor near the door with one of the bed's blankets, asleep before I can ask any question.

Oddly, I feel no fear of Yunnus. He is from a Christian family, and I have already seen and smelled and felt and known the very possible worst that the presence of men can subject me to. We have a second arduous day, this time on the back donkey paths only for the morning. After stopping at Qardaha for a meal of bread and fruit, Yunnus turns the donkey toward the west and then south, in the direction of Jablah. On the second night we sleep east of there, in a village called Al Muaysirah.

It is mid-May now, and the air warms more each day, though the night air is cool. When we reach the coast we are welcomed at a safe house in Baniyas. Here we are provided separate rooms, and I luxuriate in my privacy. I have never slept alone before and while I feel secure, I miss my little sister next to me. Yet, I think of the rare opportunity this provides and decide to enjoy it. The Orthodox family serves us a breakfast so ample, my eyes bulge at the waste: stuffed cabbage and bread, eggs fried with tomatoes and greens is too much for my morning stomach. The woman laughs and packs up a basket of the hot cabbage and rice, along with cold bulgar salad, olives, bread, and grapes. We gobble this down for lunch, stopping along the road outside Tartous. From Tartous, we redirect, going east back toward the mountains and turn southwest before the road to Homs. I have never been south of Ladehkiya before and am learning so much about my country. I wish I could tell Marta…

Yunnus had diligently studied a map with his uncle. When no one is near, he pulls the map from his pocket and shares with me names of cities and towns we will pass. We continue our journey, now moving away from the road to Beyruth and arrive, after more arduous mountain climbing but this time on a true road, at a

Christian village called Na-isiyah. I will remain in the household of a missionary family while Yunnus travels alone to Beyruth to secure passage on a freighter. I do not mind.

CHAPTER 17

MISSIONARIES

Southern Syria - May 1914

MARY

Again, I have a room all to myself. To sleep, to think, to brush my hair with a silver brush that beckons to me from the dresser table. Best of all, I enjoy this couple, Musa and Sarah, who laugh at the supper table with their children. Imagine!

They are Protestants, like me. They have been trained by the missionaries in Beyruth and are now settled to do their work in this town of Wadi al-Nasara, the Valley of Christians. Sarah is so kind to me, and it surprises me how easily I talk with her. They work with other Armenians and many converted Druze Syrians, too. They tell me they know a family that moved to Amirka and that is the family that is helping me escape. Musa confirms it must be Yunnus and

Boutris' relatives. So, all these strangers who do not know me have conspired to help me. I am humbled and overwhelmed. That night, in my bed, I cry, again, but this time with gratitude.

Sarah and Musa are short in stature, very short. Their faces crinkle when they laugh, and I witness a true jolliness for the first time. I think of my father's face: not necessarily stern, yet typically stoic and serious, at times deeply solemn. He was overwhelmed with responsibility and expectations, of himself and of others, including me. When, in the summers, the greater family gathered at Kaladouran, only then did I see Hayrig loosen and laugh. But on a typical day he held the world on his shoulders. How shocking, utterly devastating it must have been for him to fail at holding me from those Turkish dogs. Enough! No more thoughts of home.

My face is turning to an unknown future, and it begins here at Sarah's kitchen table. She is teaching me some English words each day. I will need to master this fourth language and not a word in Turkish, Armenian, or Arabic can help me. The days fly by and I practice my new phrases while helping Sarah with wash and cooking. When Yunnus returns on the 12th day, I am a tiny bit disappointed, not ready to end my days in this charming place. But there is no choice. Indeed, never have I had any choice to make in my life and would hardly know how to make one now. I hold Sarah tight, thinking of her as a mother I've not been raised with, but fortune provided to me for these few days. By morning, we are on the road again, this time accompanied by Musa, who will return with the donkey and cart for safekeeping and sharing among their network of Syria's helpers.

There is one more night to sleep on Syrian soil, in Beyruth. I am elated to be greeted by an American missionary. Eassa Wolcott is the leader of the Syrian missionaries and has even visited the missions in Kessab and Ladehkiya! He pronounces my city with hard consonants like the Syrians do: Lat-takia. He has arranged the passage for us to France and then all the way to New York and warns us not to listen if any ticket agents say the passage is not valid. (They try to do this and sell a new ticket.) We are given rooms at the Mission House in Beyruth, larger than the missions I have known. I so wish Marta could see.

When at last we climb the gangplank to the ship, I look back only once. When the ship pulls away and heads northwest, I strain my eyes from the deck, imagining I can see all the way up the coastline to Ladehkiya, holding Marta in its grasp, and pray for her. My sister is a jubilant soul, and oh, so innocent. Can she be strong? Uneasily, I admit to myself that I doubt her ability to adapt. I pray I am wrong. My thought turns to my father. What would he think of me traveling across the world to join my brothers? Unheard of...

Why, the household would collapse without me. Ah, but I am forgetting. There is no household. Best not to think of it or which Turkish dog may be this night sleeping in the bedroom I shared with Marta. The ship is now too far into the ocean to see the northern coast.

"Goodbye, dear Marta," I whisper to the wind and turn my face to the open sea.

When we reach Marseille I strain my memory for French words to practice. Yunnus and I need no longer pretend to be married. On this ship we are brother and sister. There are many people on board from other countries and private circumstances are not discussed. We do not have two cabins, as we will have on the Atlantic crossing, but we each have a berth. Food is not included in fourth-class, and we have brought a large basket prepared by Sarah and added to by the Mission house staff. The remaining supplies from our cart are contributions to the mission. I am impressed to think of the process by which these people have carefully arranged our journey and also connected across the land. I will remember them all in my prayers and carry their faces in my heart.

We carry papers that I do not read, prepared by Eassa Wolcott and stamped, and they seem to offer a sort of magical ease. We are not bothered by hustlers and agents and easily disembark in Marseille, a city so much larger than Ladehkiya yet similar to Beyruth on the port side. Yunnus speaks a fair command of French—he is quite educated like most Syrians raised in the mission schools—and navigates a path directly to the train depot and the proper train track. We do not sleep until we are on board the train and we wake hours later, in Paris, the city of light and wonder. I cannot imagine how one would live here; it is so overwhelming that I choose to look but little. We change from one station to another on a trolley car, and then we are on yet another train before even one full day has worn itself out.

The following morning, the *SS Rochambeau* awaits us, and I believe I will faint when I see it. Here we must write our names on a ledger, and I tremble to think of writing in English. Yunnus takes the quill and writes it for me, while I study the letter over his hand. Mary Simon, seventeen. Housemaid. From Turkey. Syrian. I try not to feel anger at this last. I cannot make out the word he puts for address, but I see for last relative he writes Boutros and a long surname. It is done. I am listed as single, and I have my own tiny cabin. We are in a better class and meals are provided. I overhear someone say the date, June 6th, and Yunnus says the crossing will take nine or ten days.

We stand at the rail for many hours after the shoreline recedes from Le Havre. This time I am reluctant to turn and face the wind and my future. Not just yet. I try to conjure up that long ago, late afternoon of panic, when Hovsep fled home and I hurriedly packed food for him and Asadour. The sun was setting upon the stone wall outside the garden, the boys being whisked away under cover of darkness to the piers by Father and Uncle Hagop. I try with all my ability to picture Hovsep's face, but I fail. Asadour, even less. I was eight then. I loved my brothers. But much has passed since. I have cooked and cleaned and seen to Marta and to Hayrig for so many years now, then plunged into Hell. No! I will not think. Nor will I try to remember more, no more than I can imagine my future—a future with a stranger.

In New York, we pass through the largest, and tallest, room I have ever seen, waiting in queues between iron railings holding hundreds of people. After hours of shuffling through the lines, it takes less than a minute to be looked over and papers handed back. Then, the loudest streets imaginable, buildings so tall the streets are like tunnels between them, a beautiful station, then we are quickly on a train. Crossing a river, passing through fields and pastures. The place is called New York still, but the land outside our window looks like endless patches of various fabrics, mostly very green and with the largest trees I have ever seen. My eyes close. At a station in another large city, Yunnus gently awakens me at the shoulder.

"Mary, we are at Syracuse. We will step off the train for a rest. Here I will leave you. Do you remember? I will meet cousins, will stay in this place to work. But you will have a companion. Come, we must meet someone. Keep this ticket, and leave your bag here..."

We step down from the car and sit on a platform bench. I am so afraid to take my eyes from the passenger car, afraid it will leave me there. But we are sitting only five minutes when,

"Mary! Barev, my cousin!"

I wheel my head around to locate the voice, vaguely familiar to my ears.

"What?" And then, he is embracing me. It is Asadour! Not my brother, but my cousin, Asadour. I am surprised how well I remember him. Yet after all, he has only been away three years. My heart soars as I sink into the arms of family.

Back on the train, Asadour talks non-stop, after attempting to ask me questions, which I promptly shut down. My decision is made. There is no point to talk about Hell. There is no man on the earth who can comprehend it and no point for me to relive it. I choose instead my future. I am returned from death and given life again. God is so good. So I listen to Asadour: his school in Rochester; the Churukian boys (Do I remember? Yes, of course I do); cousin Bhogos, Aunt Mary's son; the courses they have studied. And he has seen Hovsep! He traveled to a big lake to inform Hovsep of my plight and put the wheels in motion. And he has seen Manas and Khatchig! I will see them too, after just a day and a night on the train. He is taking me to Detroit where my lost family of brothers awaits me. God is so good!

In Detroit, Michigan, we sit in a living room with many people. I have clung too much already to Hovsep, Manas, and Khatchig. They are so good to look at, although I can hardly recognize Hovsep. He looks like an old man with hair whiter than snow, whiter than the grey hairs of Father! There is a man I vaguely recognize, too, Nageeb, but cannot yet place from where. Hovsep's wife, Helen, is pretty, so short, and clearly from a poor village. She holds onto a one-year-old child named Henna and also cradles a newborn of just one month! An older couple is introduced: Eassa and Mary Simon. They are responsible for my rescue—one of my brothers leans in to whisper this in my ear—for the missionaries who located me. I study their faces. I wonder how much they know… of me.

And then someone—I don't know who, exactly—points across the carpet to the far side of the room, points at a dark-haired man sitting stiffly, tall and straight, and says, "That is the man you will marry. In four months' time."

CHAPTER 18

NEW COUNTRY

Detroit - July 1914

JOE

Joe stepped off the train in Highland Park and walked the few blocks to the Simon home on Victor Avenue. The surrounding whistles and shouts combined man-made sounds with machine noises—squeals and horns of streetcars—and the more natural clicks of horseshoes striking against brick and hardpacked dust. The scene resonated instantly and plunged Joe's thoughts backward. He found himself contemplating past impressions of cities. The first had been Ladehkiya (or Lat-takia), with guttural Arab words, at first unfamiliar, shouted all about him from vendors and authority figures. Thoughts of Marseilles and Paris drifted through his consciousness with less awareness, just as he had drifted through them as if he were an insect passing through; the effect could not enter his pores, let alone hold him hostage. By contrast, New York City made the most impact; it had assaulted his senses with a sort of hostility. Perhaps, it was mostly fear, he now acknowledged, but still, offensive to his very soul.

Detroit is a little different, he mused. He hated being trapped within the confines of any city. That much was clear, now that he had experienced the sensation of having the best of both worlds. His small acreage high on a hill in Port Hune, with its modest but warm farmhouse, was a haven from which he felt privileged to descend each day, in order to work at the salt block—a small price to pay. A city, true, but Port Hune felt more like a small town, like even Kessab center, with goods available, also work, yet manageable. He was not immersed within it, even when accessing its benefits. Detroit was a true city, he thought. And, like New York, full of new people from old countries. But here, only the noise and suffocation of its size bothered him. It was not hostile. It just was what it was. He would simply have to readjust to it for a few months. For his sister.

"Kee-fek, Yussef," said Mary Simon, as she ushered him through the doorway of the Simon flat. Then she practiced her English, "Yoo ahr wel'kum heer," and giggled like a girl.

He followed her into the parlor, armed with purpose and looking forward to interacting with the

Simons again. There was a wedding to plan. Meanwhile, Joe would move his family back to the city for the summer months, so that Mary could be present and able to participate. Helen had pointed out, along with Eassa Simon, that it was unfair to keep her locked away in a northern city until her wedding day. And he knew well that until then, his household was the only suitable place for her to live. Unconsciously, they were all trying to make life feel as normal for her as possible, he supposed. Was that possible? He could not know the answer, and so he shrugged, determined to focus on whatever details might require his attention. First, and foremost, he must establish work. He did not want to lose his piece of heaven at Port Hune and could not afford to lose income during this period. With a new mouth to feed, too.

Helen will enjoy the break to show off the newborn Jirgis to old friends and female company, he was thinking, as Eassa Simon entered the room and interrupted his musing.

"Sit, Youssef! We have much goodness to celebrate and even more to plan for."

"And I have news for you, too," Najeeb, added, appearing from behind his father. "Ford Company has a position for you, in the mailroom. You will come with me, tomorrow!" Joe looked up, grateful, but hesitant.

He started to say something, but thought better of it, and closed his lips. It would wait until tomorrow.

The following Sunday, Helen, Mary, Henna, and tiny Jirgis would accompany him to the house on Kendall Street, where Khatchig and Manas lived on the upper floor and they were to settle in on the floor below. Joe collected all the garden produce that could be stuffed into a basket manageable for Mary to handle, and he lugged their three suitcases. Helen handled the two children and her own basket of supper. He had given away produce to his colleagues at the plant and arranged for some of them to tend the garden and help themselves throughout the remaining months. He planned to return by harvest, to slide back into the plant kitchen and resume his job. He was assured by the kitchen boss that few could rival his baking. So, armed with return plans, Joe joined his growing family on the train, determined to look forward to the coming months.

Sitting across from his sister on the facing train bench, Joe gazed at her thoroughly for the first time since her arrival, trying to be as discreet as possible. There had been few hours between planning, negotiating, arranging, and welcoming the birth of the second boy. He finally found himself floating in a moment that seemed carved out for undistracted thought to the red-haired beauty before him. Sister Mary. He had last seen her when hiding beneath a grapevine, shaking uncontrollably, pulled from there by four sets of masculine hands that carted him off to the docks. But not before Mary had shoved a nondescript canvas sack onto his shoulder, which he had later opened to find shankleesh cheese, olive pighah bread, and tightly wrapped grapeleaves stuffed with meat and rice— enough protein to get two brothers through their first day thrust out of the world they knew. Ten years ago. He strained to visualize her then, a girl between eight and nine years, planted at the kitchen stove, who should instead be in school with her brothers.

In this country, her beauty would have been a blessing for her; in the old country it was a curse, he realized with a jolt. He filled with shame, not only for leaving her behind—however little control he had in the matter—but for hardly thinking of her since, while navigating among a new world of communities and the business of building his family. He wondered what Khatchig and Manas thought about it. They had been cared for by their little sister for about six years after he left Syria—well into her teens, when she might have been educated, or even married before…. Stop! He argued with himself. She would not want his pity, he felt sure. She would not wish to speak of her tragedy, even if he had the courage to ask. Though he knew

Mary little, somehow he knew this of her—only God knows how.

The marriage seemed right, Joe told himself, his thoughts switching seamlessly to the future. But why does she not ask even one question? What is it about her that shows no curiosity about her very own future? It occurred to him that he, himself, had asked no questions when confronted with upheaval between worlds...of impossible facts and certain pain. He had no wish to trigger these in her. His father—their father... no, he couldn't ask that either.

"Mari-jan, are you feeling well?" The question felt limp, unworthy. He could do no more.

"Of course, Hovsep." Hearing his birth name from a woman's lips in the new country was so odd to his ears, he realized he had only heard it spoken by his brothers. "I am rested and certainly well fed by my sister-in-law." She nodded respectfully to Helen, whose face was, surprisingly, unreadable. Mary then looked at him, right in the eye, and managed a smile which was no more revealing than his wife's face.

He wondered at the relationship between the women. Was it tense? Like with Manas? Poor Helen had begun their married life together saddled with his brother's shock and anger at his bad fortune, and his surly recovery while he awaited the fake leg. Joe felt pity for his wife and wondered how it was, sharing her current life with this sister, whose nature he knew nothing of. He could not guess. He managed nothing more, but snuck one more look at his sister, and sighed.

She would not be forthcoming. There was something of relief in that fact. Joe felt this but could not analyze the thought as a feeling. It was reality. How could anyone receive what she might have to share? Would he want to know? Certainly not. But she is safe. She is safe, he told himself again. She will be Ameen's wife and well cared for. There is no need to think any further than that. She is safe. And Marta? Asadour had heard that she is safe at school in Beyruth and with Nishan for weekends. That was all the thinking Joe could manage for now.

Gratefully, the train approached Detroit and the business of living would soon replace all this thinking about things he could not control. As he and his wife and sister carried belongings into the home, Khatchig and Manas greeted them in the stairwell with embraces and smiles, snatching baskets from the women's arms. Khatchig affectionately tousled the black hair of one-year-old Henna, who managed to walk up the steps all by himself.

"Your timing is perfect!" gushed Manas. "The American holiday is tomorrow. We will all picnic at the lake where the sky will light up with the big sparkles." He glanced at Mary to assess the impact of his announcement and was rewarded with a smile.

Joe looked carefully at his brothers. Khatchig and Manas, a.k.a. Archie and Leo, were solid, easy in their skin, he thought. He filled with gladness that they had come to the new country to settle. He thought of his other two brothers, one back home, the other—only God knows where—and of Marta. Then Hovsep Karamardian, a.k.a. Joe Peter, moved his eyes from his old family to his new family, Haloun, a.k.a. Helen, Henna, a.k.a. John, and Jirgis, a.k.a. George.

We gonna be okay, he told his heart. And allowed himself a silent prayer for the others, wherever they were.....

EPILOGUE

IDENTITY

Ithaca, New York - February 2021

AUTHOR

I awake early, before the first light, and as I turn my head on the pillow, my eyes fall upon the lights of the mine from across the lake. They are twinkling back at me through the glass in my window frame, brightening the darkness like fireworks that are frozen permanently as they descend back to the earth. My house sits atop South Hill, several miles south of the lake's tip, with a perfect view of Cayuga Lake snaking north until it bends and continues, stretching away from Myers Park on the east shore, Taughannock Park on the west. I can see the salt mine from my bed, and this morning it holds my attention. I grab the binoculars from the windowsill and adjust the lens to scan the shoreline up close, noticing that the mine's buildings layer up the slope from the water to the hilltop. Some structures have the same light patterns and I imagine them to be identical warehouses with outside floodlights spaced exactly the same. To their left along the bottom shore, there is a mysterious cluster of red lights that seem to be something specific, and at the water's edge, appears some sort of lit barge. This is the modern Rock Salt Company, now called Cargill. It grew out of the original salt works that burned down in 1962, a mile to the north, where my ancestors had met and worked.

When Jido died, I was impressionable, romantic, and in some way, haunted. I often imagined myself being seen through his eyes, whether or not with approval. Occasionally, I felt I heard messages from him in short phrases, sending me guidance. There was an experience I could not deny, yet never managed to wrap my head around. So I made a point not to think about it over the years, since it made me uncomfortable to recall.

Between my junior and senior year in high school, my friends Rick and Genelle, threw me a birthday party. I arrived with my boyfriend to Rick's second-floor apartment above his family home. Rick's five siblings also attended. The family was into séances and decided to conduct one with their Ouija board; they were all seated on the living room floor, surrounding a table wedged between sofas. I was a bit freaked out and tried to hide this from everyone, standing aside as far as possible from the enclosure of sofas and the table holding the Ouija board. Later in the game the table suddenly lurched and seemed to fly quickly in my direction. Startled, I jumped out of the way and backed against the wall.

One of the sisters said, "Denice, it's for you!"

Oh no, I thought, no way I'm in this thing! I backed away from the room and into the kitchen, hoping they would move on to some other focus. I wanted no part.

"Denice, it's your grandfather." They were spelling out messages from tapping or something. I froze, not trusting their words, but stunned nonetheless at the mention of Jido.

"He says go home now. Your mother needs you!"

I did not believe for one moment that my grandfather was sending me a message through a Ouija board. Yet I watched myself head to the door, gathering up presents on my way while my boyfriend wordlessly swooped me out the door and down the outside staircase to drive me home at breakneck speed. When I walked through the backdoor of our white ranch house the first thing I saw was my mother's back. She was uncharacteristically frozen in a chair, staring silently out the front picture window. She did not move or seem to consciously hear our arrival. Had she heard me enter? She remained eerily motionless.

"Mom?" I was almost afraid to speak, fear gripping me. I dropped my gifts and exchanged glances with my boyfriend.

She turned her head towards us slowly, as if in a trance, and took her time to speak.

"My mother is gone." It was a whisper, her lips barely working.

My grandmother lived far away in Lincoln, Nebraska. I had never in my entire life seen my mother like this; somber, subdued. I'd seldom even seen her unhappy, if ever. I realized then that my father was away, installing his latest receiver project at a radio observatory in Puerto Rico. She was all alone, learning that her own mother was gone from the world and taking it in by herself. I ran to her.

After that I was on the lookout for messages. Mostly they didn't come, but I did sense Jido's presence at times. My college experience was the intense immersion at a music conservatory in Boston and on the few free days available, I found myself wandering Watertown and Somerville Streets, searching for Armenian faces and hoping for some sort of clue…of what, I could not imagine. These were the communities that housed Armenian groceries, bookstores, even clubs sprinkled throughout the various neighborhoods. The highlight of senior year at New England Conservatory is a senior recital which typically takes both semesters to prepare. Due to the memory of that anxious time, I can call to mind the date of my recital faster than that of my own wedding. On March 23rd, 1975, I stood on stage in the crook of the grand piano, feeling rather nervous in my floor-length Gunny Saks dress, and scoured the audience for my parents' faces. But after the first introductory interlude, when I opened my mouth to sing it was Jido I felt watching me, raining beams of pride. I sang for him.

In the early 1980s, my career now anchored in New York City, I took time to stroll Atlantic Avenue in Brooklyn for the many Armenian businesses I had heard about. Shops had bright colored signs, some in the alphabet that was foreign to me. The avenue was long and wide and the Armenian area was very consolidated and easy to cover, unlike those in the Boston suburbs. My pulse sped up automatically at the recognition of any of these storefronts. I entered some of them and tried to strike up a conversation with the owners. They were gracious, if a little puzzled at my apparent ignorance of the culture. I sensed that whenever I mentioned that my grandfather was Armenian, they might nod with the unspoken understanding that I may be curious, but not a real, full-blooded Armenian. I bought albums of Armenian music and played one of them so often

I memorized most of the songs long before I learned anything about Komitas, the signature composer of the Armenian culture. My favorite was called Groong (Ka – roonk), about a crane that is longing for the homeland. The sentiment, the melody, the consonants and vowels of the syllables that I did not understand expressed for me my own deep longing to understand what it was to be Armenian. Decades later I would sing the song in concert, but for now it was a secret, contained inside my lower east side apartment, between me, my soul, and the unknown.

Michael Arlen wrote in his memoir, "I often wonder what it really is to be Armenian in our world—what message it is that we Armenians carry down from our journey through the centuries." I wondered what my dad would say to this.

On a sunny spring weekend my parents were in the city to attend a banquet and stayed at a Manhattan hotel. Mom and I took a walk under a striking blue sky through midtown while Dad napped. I loved the luxury of having them to myself (a rare occurrence) and looked forward to leisurely conversation. When we returned to the hotel, I got my chance.

My father was the family ambassador. To some he was peacemaker, mentor to others. He was the "forever" glue that held the greater family together, navigating personalities, negotiating grudges, and hosting reunions and gatherings. Half a dozen cousins from both sides of my family cycled through our home, living with us for some period of time and challenge: sometimes, trouble at home or estrangement from their own parents. Coming to "Uncle George" became a common solution. My siblings and I were so accustomed to sharing our parents, I never thought twice about it until, as an older adult visiting on a limited time schedule, I had to grapple with the impatience of having to fit myself into Dad's busy schedule.

Now he sat in the overstuffed green chair by the window. He never looked like he was lounging exactly. He did not slump, but always seemed casually comfortable, usually with one knee tucked up under his chin and a foot resting on the chair. He was one of those people who felt right in their skin, neither self-conscious nor elitist, but humbly appropriate in any setting. He and I meandered into a philosophical conversation that bordered on the spiritual and eventually came around to the topic of family.

I was burning with questions that I didn't have enough knowledge to formulate, but I heard myself ask, "Dad, do you ever dream of your ancestors?"

"If you mean wonder, yes. Of course, I know nothing but the first name of my two grandfathers. But like you, I feel them stir from somewhere deep inside." As usual, he used his hands, slicing through the room's atmosphere to emphasize his words, and we discussed it awhile. Then he lowered his voice and said, "Honey, I believe with all my heart that you and I hold the seed of our ancestors in our souls. We are the carriers and meant to be the messengers."

I did not doubt it for a moment; I felt it, too.

An enduring family tale that floated in our family for as long as I recall, one I knew well before Jido died and bequeathed to me an identity crisis, was my favorite: Jido arrived at the salt flats north of Ithaca by complete accident. He never did pronounce a 'th' and had intended to buy a ticket to Utica, a city in central New York with a strong community of Middle Easterners and plenty of factory jobs. The train conductor thought he said, "Itaka, tank you very much." But when he arrived at the train station on Ithaca's inlet, a Syrian boy he had met onboard told him, "You need a job? Come with me!" and led him to the local train and on up the lake to the International Salt Company. There, the bosses recognized that he could communicate with the Syrian crews and immediately made him a straw boss, not a popular move with said crews.

Uncle John told me, "They hated his guts!" And he loved to repeat his mother's words, "They forbade me to go near the *Armine*, so I told them 'Nah, I hate his guts,' but I knew I would marry him, first time I saw him!"

The Syrians called my Jido, '*Bete Armine*': Pete, the Armenian. I learned this while interviewing three aging Abraham sisters several decades ago. They were still living in the little home on Syrian Hill (Tubbha, to them) where they'd grown up. On that day, they shared much about their childhood Tubbha. And they remembered 'Bete Armine.'

I stare across the water now from my bed, thinking how different the original salt production must have been. The operation that employed my grandparents used the salt well method: brine formed by water was pumped up and piped into boilers to be evaporated into fine table salt. Onondaga Indians were seen making salt with brine and kettles in 1653 by the missionary Le Moyne. The first well at Myers was sunk in 1891 and another in 1892. By 1904, the salt works at Salt Point that Joe Peter Karamardian arrived to work at five years later, had four wells, fifteen boilers, six grainers, and two vacuum pans spread through nine buildings on Salt Point. All of this encompassed the flats just north of the park, employing as many as one hundred twenty workers. Most of these were Syrian immigrants, sprinkled with some Ukranians and other Eastern Europeans.

My eyes follow the shoreline jutting northwest to Myers Park where I know Salt Point is tucked just behind the low lighthouse. Stories fill my head of Jido traveling across continents and oceans and islands. These are the seeds of my own confidence in the world. I absorbed them like fairy tales, miracles of life and perseverance. They informed me of my own abilities: the unshakeable conviction that anything is possible.

True, I would encounter self-doubt at various times in a life, like any, of ebbs and flows. But I began grounded, in possibility and faith, part of a tribe— something larger than myself. Once again, I grab the binoculars and follow the coastline left from the large mine operation to that abandoned, tree-lined point where Hovsep Bedros Karamardian became Joseph Peter and planted the world I know.

I wanted badly to know how he got here. What if my twelve-year-old self had known it would take a lifetime to put it together? Thank God, impossibility hadn't yet occurred to me. With the fearlessness of youth, I simply presumed I would find it.

Joe and Helen Peter

Generations to follow, see family trees on pages
232-235

Generations Out of Syria

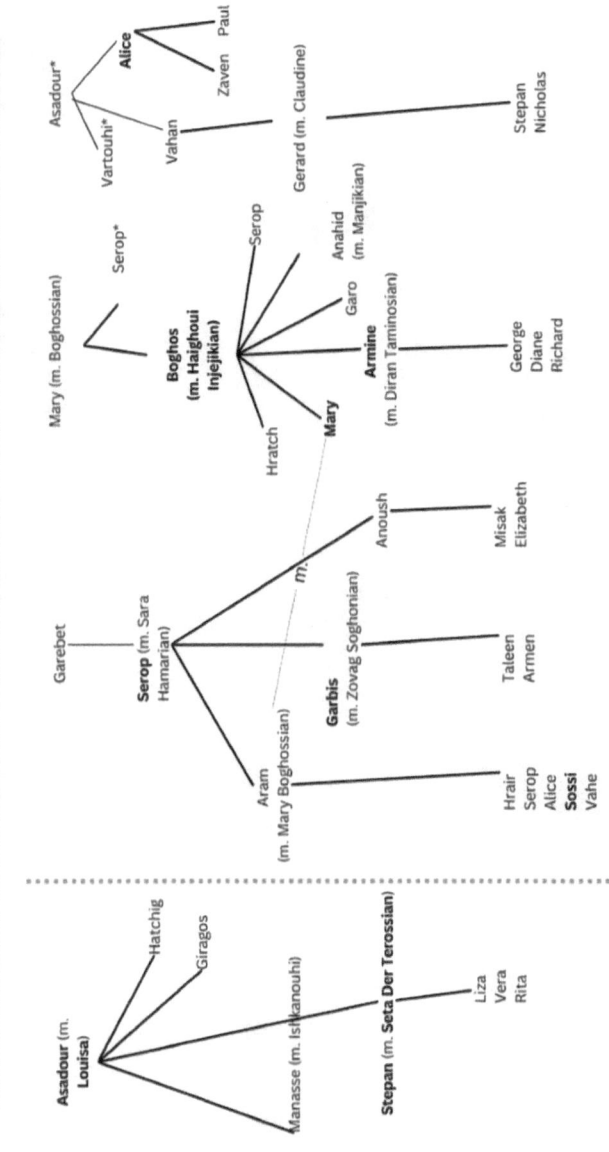

Giragos*

Hatchig*

Asadour (m. **Louisa**)
— Hatchig
— Giragos
— Manasse (m. Ishkanouhi)
— **Stepan** (m. **Seta Der Terossian**)
  — Liza
  — Vera
  — Rita

Garebet

Serop (m. Sara Hamarian)
— Aram (m. Mary Boghossian)
  — Hrair
  — Serop
  — Alice
  — **Sossi**
  — Vahe
— **Garbis** (m. Zovag Soghonian)
  — Taleen
  — Armen
— Anoush
  — Misak
  — Elizabeth

Mary (m. Boghossian)
— Serop*

Boghos (m. **Haighoui Injejikian**)
— Hratch
— **Mary**
— **Armine** (m. Diran Taminosian)
  — George
  — Diane
  — Richard
— Garo
— Anahid (m. Manjikian)
— Serop

Vartouhi*

Asadour*
— **Alice**
  — Zaven
  — Paul
— Vahan (m. Gerard (m. Claudine))
  — Stepan
  — Nicholas

m.

Bedros Line

BEDROS KARAMARDIAN AND TZAGHIR INJEJIKIAN

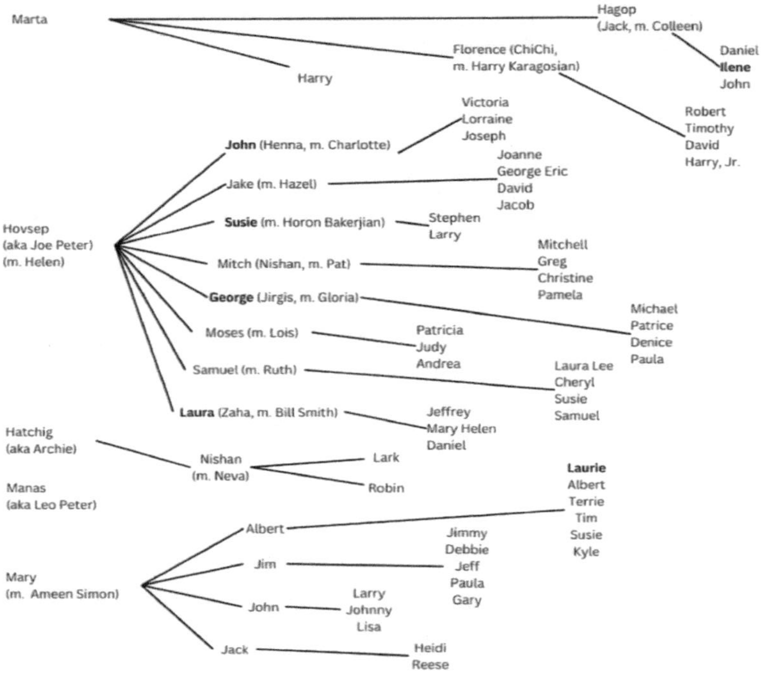

Marta

Harry

Hovsep
(aka Joe Peter)
(m. Helen)

Hatchig
(aka Archie)

Manas
(aka Leo Peter)

Mary
(m. Ameen Simoni)

Hagop
(Jack, m. Colleen)

Florence (ChiChi,
m. Harry Karagosian)

John (Henna, m. Charlotte)

Jake (m. Hazel)

Susie (m. Horon Bakerjian)

Mitch (Nishan, m. Pat)

George (Jirgis, m. Gloria)

Moses (m. Lois)

Samuel (m. Ruth)

Laura (Zaha, m. Bill Smith)

Nishan
(m. Neva)

Lark

Robin

Albert

Jim

John

Jack

Victoria
Lorraine
Joseph

Joanne
George Eric
David
Jacob

Stephen
Larry

Patricia
Judy
Andrea

Jeffrey
Mary Helen
Daniel

Jimmy
Debbie
Jeff
Paula
Gary

Larry
Johnny
Lisa

Heidi
Reese

Daniel
Ilene
John

Robert
Timothy
David
Harry, Jr.

Mitchell
Greg
Christine
Pamela

Michael
Patrice
Denice
Paula

Laura Lee
Cheryl
Susie
Samuel

Laurie
Albert
Terrie
Tim
Susie
Kyle

GLOSSARY

NAMES, PLACES AND THINGS IN ODAR WITH VARIOUS SPELLINGS

Amirka; (pronunciation for America by first generation Armenians)

Kessab, Kasap, Kesap, Casab, Casbis; town northwesternmost in Syria, on Turkish border, until years was exclusively, and is still predominantly, Armenian; named Casabelle and Casabella by first Crusaders

Latakia, Lattakia, Ladehkiya
(Kessabtsi pronunciation), Al Ladhiqiyah Port City in Northwest Syria; ancient name Laodice

Kaladouran, Karadouran; coastal village of Kessab, northwest Syria on border with Turkey

Beirut, Beyruth, Beyrout; major city in Lebanon

Tartus, Tartous

Junieh, Jounieh

Port Hune (pronunciation of Port Huron by first
generation Syrians, Armenians) in Michigan, U.S.

Itaka, Ithaca (pronunciation by Joe Peter) in Finger
Lakes region of New York on Cayuga Lake

J'abal A'qra, Jebbel Akra, Mount Cassius; mountain
of Kessab

Jabal Mussa, Musa Dagh, Kizil Dagh; name for
mountain and village of and near Kessab

Ishkenderun, Alexandretta; (modern name) city in
Turkey near border of Syria

Aintab; Gaziantep (Turkish name)

Constantinople; Istanbul (modern name)

Melkia, B'Melki, kfar melki; costal village near Lebanon
(residents called themselves Syrian circa 1900)

Barlum Monastery, Ballum, Barlahoy, Barlaam;
(believed to be founded by St. Barlaam)

Legion d'Orient, Armenian Leggionaires, Gamovar; names for the group of Armenian fighters WW1

Gamovar; volunteers, freedom fighters in Kessab after the war who patrolled and protected Kessab area

Shushan, Shoushan (Lily, name in Armenian and Hebrew)

Elisa, Alice

Armine, Armenouhi, (Armen, male version)

Asadour, Asadur

Ameen (family spelling), Amin (usual Arabic spelling)

Bedros, Boutris, Bete, Peter; Armenian, Greek, Arabic, English versions

Hovsep, Youssef, Youssif, Jose, Joseph, Joe; Armenian, Arabic, Spanish, English versions

Khatchig, Hatchig, Archie

Boghos, Paul

Laura, Zaha, Zahia, Zahea, Florence (meaning flower, Arabic versions)

Henna, Hana, John

Manas, Manasse, Leo

Moses, Mose, Mussa, Moussa, Moosey (nickname in Peter family)

Marta, Martha

Mary, Mariam, Maryam

Louise, Louisa, Louiza, Lousine

Nishan, Nishon, Mitchell

George, Giragos (Armenian), Jirgis (Syrian)

Yunnus, Younus, Yunus (Arabic) Yunis (Greek)

Tzaghir, Dzaghir, Tsaghig, Kitcha, Haigha, Zarig, Zaghig; (meaning flower, Armenian version female)

Kamor, Ataturk; 1923 took control as leader of Turkey

Kibbe, kibbee, kibbeh, kufta (Armenian version); baked mix of lamb with pine nuts and bulgar

Lubi, loobi; green bean and tomato stew, usually with chunks of lamb

Lamajoun, lamajoon, Lahmajoun; meat pies on flat bread made with ground meat, onions and peppers

Koussa, kousa, cusa (squash, zucchini, usually stuffed with meat and rice)

Babagnoush, babaganoush (eggplant)

Shadiyeh; Arabic word for pilaf

Shankleesh, tchingleesh; a cheese spiced and coated with zatar, a middle Eastern spice

Sourkig , Armenian pizza

Dolma, dolmades (Greek) tolma, sarma (Armenian); rolled grapeleaves, stuffed with meat and rice

Pigegh; Armenian olive oil bread twisted in knot shapes

Baklava, paklava; type of pastry layers with nuts and syrup, cut into diamond shapes

Boorma; version of baklava with nuts and syrup inside rolled pastry layers and cut in cigar shapes

Smeed; pastry cake made with farina

Hayrig; Armenian for father

Mayrig; Armenian for mother

Jihdo, Jido, Jid, Jidi; Arabic for grandfather, my grandfather (our version Jido)

Jida, Jidehti, Sito; Arabic for grandmother (our version, Sito)

Shukran, shookran; Arabic for thank you

Yallah, yella; Arabic for come on, let's go

Kee-fek, kee-fik; Arabic hello

Huffla, mahrajan; Syrian festival

Effendi; man of education in Ottoman Empire

Gendarme; officer of authority, such as police

Tonir; oven

Odar; Armenian for "other, stranger, foreigner"

Jan; a term of endearment in Armenian, i.e. Louisa-jan
or Stepan Jan (i.e. Louisa, dear)

Inch bes es?; Armenian for How are you?

Shad lav em, park asdouzo; Armenian for I am fine,
thank you.

Barev; Armenian for Hello

Medz Yeghem; "Great Evil Crime" (Armenian)

Last names connected to or associated with Karamardian
family: Injejikian, Aslanian, Giragossian, Chalakian,
Margosian, Karagozian, Karagosian, Titizian,
M'gerditchian, Boghossian, Churukian, Sarkissian,
Apelian, Terterian, Ashekian, Nazarian, Kakusian,
Asarian, Hasessian, Ayanian, Berber

BIBLIOGRAPHY AND RECOMMENDED READING

Arlen, Michael J. *Passage to Ararat.* Farrar, Strauss and Giroux, 1975.

Balakian, Peter. *The Black Dog of Fate.* Basic Books, 1997.

Balakian, Peter. *The Burning Tigris: The Armenian Genocide and America's Response.* Harper Collins, 2003.

Bohjalian, Chris. *Sandcastle Girls.* Knopf Doubleday Publishing Group, 2013.

Edgarian, Carol. *Rise the Euphrates.* Random House, 1994.

Hovannisian, Richard G. *The Republic of Armenia, Volumes 1 – 4.* Univ. of California Press, 1971.

Hovannisian, Richard G. *Armenian People from Ancient to Modern Times Vols I and II.* Palgrave MacMillan US, 1997.

Kessab Educational Association. *Kessab and the Kessabtsis: Special edition commemorating 50th anniversary.* KEA of LA, Calif, USA, 2011.

Marcom, Micheline Aharonian. *Three Apples Fell From Heaven, A Novel.* Riverhead Books, a member of Penguin Putnam, Inc., 2001.

Mouradian, Khatchig. *Resistance Network: The Armenian Genocide and Humanitarianism in Ottoman Syria 1915-1918.* Michigan State University Press, 2021.

Morganthau, Henry. *Ambassador Morganthau's Story; A Personal Account of the Armenian Genocide.* Original publish date 1918. Reprinted with Edwin Mellen Press, 2022.

Pattie, Susan Paul. *The Armenian Legionnaires: Sacrifice and Betrayal in WWI.* I.B. Tauris, 2018.

Sanjian, Avedis. *Armenian Communities in Syria under Ottoman Dominion.* Harvard University Press, 1965.

Sarkissian, Hagop. *From Kessab to Watertown: A Modern Saga*. Ohan Press, 1966.

Werfel, Frantz. *The Forty Days of Musa Dagh*. Fischer Verlag, translate David R. Godine, 1933.

Online resources

100 Years of Reformed Presbyterian Missions in Syria: Part 1 of 2 retrieved from Gentlereformation.com

Various entries retrieved from Presbyterianmission.org

Author Unknown (2015, August, 12) The Dominican Republic and its Arab Assimilation. Retrieved from Abreu Report: Global Politics.

Unpublished

George Peter. *Karamardian Kapers - personal journal writings.*

Laura Peter Smith. Various letters, 1942-1947.

NOTE ON FICTION
AND TRUTH

The **Odar** series is a work of fiction, though based on true events, true people, and mostly authentic attitude and personality. I seem to have exhausted (of my ability and to my knowledge) access to information through documented research. And I have incorporated most of what I gratefully received through first, second and third hand interviews. Yet, I fully expect additional detail to appear after publication of this work; perhaps via relatives as yet unknown to me, perhaps from less likely sources or from completely unexpected windfall. After many decades of searching and processing clues and details, nothing would surprise me.

For all the factual detail existing in *Odar,* I found it most feasible to fully share the story of Joe Peter and the settling of his several communities during historic times as a work of fiction, in order to best see the members of one family in all their human thought and action. Imagination served for certain details of action, plot and character development – gaps filled in, opinions, thoughts, and sentiments assigned. There is no way to share the material facts in my possession without some guesswork as to the heart at the center of them. I sincerely hope not to cause inconvenience to any living person via my method or for any error I may have inadvertently ascribed to real people through the telling.

I have not changed names in this story. In fact, I have taken the liberty to include real names and places gleaned from census records, passenger lists, naturalization applications, and other available documentation and assign them roles. I chose to insert real people into the lives of my ancestors where I deemed the association likely and logical, or heard mention of said persons in interviews or through family folklore. Since this telling is about real people and real places, I found little reason to fabricate in cases where names are available on record.

Finally, to quote author Yiyun Li (The New Yorker, Oct 30, 2023): "Some fiction is tamer than some life…"

I could not have expressed in a better way, the end result of the story I have laid out in these pages. Naturally, there is more than a little family drama that I have omitted. Family folklore or secrets unearthed by accident tend to exist within the fabric of most families. In this case, certain sensational details, of murder and mayhem, may well deserve their own storyline in a full volume, while detracting from this one. So yes, this work of fiction may be somewhat tamer than the complete unabridged life of Joseph Peter and/or the greater Karamardian family. But this is the story I have chosen to tell. I hope, and believe, it is enough. And that the reader has gained from the telling.

Most importantly, I dedicate this series to all of my family and to families everywhere, in all their glory and complication. And to the memory of all ancestors.

Denice Peter Karamardian

GRATITUDE RUNS DEEP

There are few words for the depth of my feelings for the primary angels of this project. First and foremost, my inspiration, my collaborator and connecting thread, a primary voice and soulmate in the journey – my late father, **George Peter,** who talked and wrote about his life and helped to access and interview first generation major characters in the book, his aunts. I dedicate every word to him, in absentia. I hope he is enjoying eternal space with the others, and the ancestors.

Sossi (Karamardian) Madzounian, my angel guide, facilitated my search and discovery with hospitality beyond belief, directed me far and wide, introduced me to the Kessab community in L.A. and continually inspires me, along with her entire family. *Ilene Karagozian Hill,* my inaugural host/guide who helped me launch discovery with graciousness, care and interest. *Lisa Bennett*, my first editor, helped shape a story line from dense quantity of material into a first draft with patience and mind blowing guidance and wisdom.

The storytellers were crucial blessings in my life to the endeavor. As witnesses, they evolved into the major character and storytellers of Odar. Their words reached out, some from final days on a sofa, others from the great beyond, to shape the world and challenges they had known and overcome: **Marta Karamardian Karagozian, Alice Karamardian Margosian, Serop Karamardian, Louisa Guzelian Karamardian, ChiChi (Florence) Karagosian, and Dr. Vahan Churukian. (The females listed here spoke in absentia.)** Their stories were augmented (and some narrated) by **Mary Boghossian Karamardian, Armine Boghossian Thomson, Seta Der Terossian Karamardian Soma, Stepan Karamardian, and Madame Rosa Karamardian**. Profound witnessing over many decades, which shaped much of the narration for the story of Odar, came from closer to home: **John Peter, Susie Peter Bakerjian, and Laura Peter Smith** (my father's siblings).

All of the above have deceased since my interviews with them. So too, have some of the second generation witnesses who provided in depth information and enhanced experience: **Gabriel Injejikian, Neva Karamardian, Harry Karagosian, Colleen Karagozian,** Cat**, Barbara and Lorraine Abraham.** I am so very grateful for the sharing of their memories of old world childhoods from *Garbis Karamardian, Anoush Karamardian Tohikian, and Kerop Kazarian*. And then of course, more miraculously appearing relatives with revelations: *Khatchig Titizian, Laurie Cunnington and the Simon sisters.*

There was much additional help from .... Gary *Lind-Sinanian* - curator, Armenian Library and Museum of America, Watertown, MA.; *Makda Watherspoon* of Cornell Arabic Department for document translations; *Kessab Educational Center*, Los Angeles, CA; *Carol Kammen*, historian, for an Ithaca initiation to research; *Lansing Historical Society and Salt Point Park exhibit; Peter Balakian*, author, for trailblazing guidance, research, and inspiration; my French translators in Paris, France *Nicholas Karamardian, Karim Bachiri, and Nadea; Jana Hextor*, medium; the *Cornell Armenian Student Association*, language classes and social support.

A very special shout out to *Steven Manley* for graphic support, *Jeffrey Smith*, for technical design (map) and technical support (photos), and once again to the very talented Sossi Madzounian for cover art (photographic for all jacket covers).

I'm grateful for additional support from cousins: *Dan and John Karagozian, Larry Bakerjian, Lark Karamardian, Alice Karamardian Vartabedian, Elo Tohikian*, and *Liza Karamardian Carter.* Also *Leslie Daniels*, author, for helpful advice and a first look at book content, *Alison Wearing*, (Stratford, Canada) memoire instructor, and my very patient friend and early copy editor, *Donna Ramer.*

Thank you to more **editors***: Kate Allyson, Brian Dooley, Ashley Swanson.* **Last, but never least**, **early readers and cheerleaders**.....*Mary Helen Myrdek, Paula Peter, Vally Kovary, Maureen Moore, Vicky Hutchinson, Michael J. Peter, Daniel Terino, Donna Ramer*, and *Patrice DiLorenzo*.

Note: names in bold represent deceased participants

ABOUT THE AUTHOR

Photo by T.C. Peter

Denice Peter Karamardian owns and operates a regional publication for Finger Lakes wine visitors and is at work on several books. She is retired from a rich tapestry of overlapping careers that spanned over forty plus years and included instructing voice, host/producer of radio concert broadcast series, fifty years of music and theater performance, columnist and reviewer. She currently lives in her hometown of Ithaca, New York (where she operated a bed and breakfast for two decades) near/ with her family.